Successful Project Managers Roadmap

Successful Project Managers Roadmap

Contents

Project Initiation 6
    1- How to start your project properly 7
    2- How to use / evaluate SWOT analysis for understanding the project better 9
    3- How to setup your project initiation 14
    4- How to create an effective project charter 16
    5- How to build an effective team 19
    6- How to conduct effective kickoff meeting 21

Project Planning 24
    1- How to perform stakeholder analysis 25
    2- How to manage a high risk project 30
    3- How to estimate more accurately 32
    4- How to plot project risks 37
    5- How to include risk factor into your estimations 39
    6- How to plan/manage project quality 41
    7- How to select outsourcing vendor effectively 43
    8- How to avoid common outsourcing pitfalls 50

Project Execution 56
    1- How to run productive and effective meetings 57
    2- How to keep everyone on the same page during the project 59
    3- How to deliver successful presentation 61
    4- How to delegate effectively 64
    5- How to motivate your team 69
    6- How to influence your team to do what you want 71

- 7- How to build trust with your client 73
- 8- How to write effective mails to your stakeholders 76

Project Monitor and Control 80

- 1- How to keep your eyes on your projects 81
- 2- How to manage remote teams 83
- 3- How to emphasize team working 85
- 4- How to manage lazy employee 88
- 5- How to manage team conflict effectively 90
- 6- How to manage project changes 100
- 7- How to prevent your project from scope creep 101
- 8- How to use Pareto Chart to improve quality 103
- 9- How to manage project issues effectively 107
- 10- How to use and apply Earned Value Management 109
- 11- How to forecast your project using Earned Value Management 114
- 12- How to assess / measure your project status and creation action plan 116
- 13- How to select appropriate management style throughout the project 118
- 14- How to manage difficult situations by persuasion techniques 122
- 15- How to manage your project when it is late 124
- 16- How to sort it out if you lied 126
- 17- How to prevent your project from failing 128

Project Closing 130

- 1- How to avoid project closing pitfalls 131
- 2- How to close your project effectively 133

Project Initiation

The Project Initiation Phase is the 1st phase in the Project Management Life Cycle, as it involves starting up a new project. You can start a new project by defining its objectives, scope, purpose and deliverables to be produced. You'll also hire your project team, setup the Project Office and review the project, to gain approval to begin the next phase.

Only with a clearly defined scope and a suitably skilled team, can you ensure success.

1- How to start your project properly

It is very important to initiate your project properly so you can continue smoothly and finish strongly, there are some actions which will protect you and help you to resolve your issues throughout the project:-

1- **Get the business knowledge:** it is your project, it is your baby who you have to know everything about its business and related worldwide field. Go and do your researches, studies and collect all information available there because it will help you during the project activities and managing change requests. Finally try to be the expert of the project business field if you can.

2- **Set the vision:** do not look at the project as it is only a product but set a vision which will surely motivate you and share that vision among your team and stakeholders.

3- **Create and Communicate Project Charter:** at this stage, project charter is the only available document which defines very high level project scope along with the budget and constraints like time and quality. Make sure that you share this project charter with your team so they can think with you from day one and alert for any issues or risks you might did not notice.

4- **Get Formal Sign off:** It is very critical step to have all documents signed off, because when things go wrong that is the only proof which will protect you.

5- **Create a Project Notebook:** Project notebook will contain all signed documents and change requests which will make it easy for anyone at any time to know everything about the project and stages it went through.

6- **Build Relationships:** without relationships with your stakeholder it will be very difficult to drive the project smoothly, because you will face a lot of situations which only good relationships will resolve it. So go and build your relationships with your client and stakeholders but make sure you can balance between professionalism and flattered.

Notes(Place Your Notes Here)

2- How to use / evaluate SWOT analysis for understanding the project better

What is SWOT analysis? (Alternatively SWOT Matrix) is a structured planning method used to evaluate the Strengths, Weaknesses, Opportunities, and Threats involved in a project or in a business venture. A SWOT analysis can be carried out for a product, place, industry or person. It involves specifying the objective of the business venture or project and identifying the internal and external factors that are favorable and unfavorable to achieving that objective.

Strengths: characteristics of the business or project that give it an advantage over others.

Weaknesses: are characteristics that place the team at a disadvantage relative to others.

Opportunities: elements that the project could exploit to its advantage.

Threats: elements in the environment that could cause trouble for the business or project

Identification of SWOTs is important because they can inform later steps in planning to achieve the objective.

How to use SWOT Analysis?

1- Create a four box matrix, with one box representing one of each of the categories of the SWOT analysis--strengths, weaknesses, opportunities and threats.

2- Hold a brainstorming meeting with other strategic planners and spend 10 to 15 minutes coming up with ideas to put in each category.

3- Observe the results of the brainstorming and write two or three things that represent the most important ideas from each category. For example, a good brand name, strong customer relationships, intellectual property rights, and supply chain access are great strengths. If the company is lacking in any of these areas, they could be large weaknesses. Opportunities often include things like new customer niches that can be tapped into, new products and technology, or new beneficial legislation. Threats could be unfavorable technology, such as a close substitute to your product or service, unfavorable regulations or bad publicity.

4- Next brainstorm ways to best take advantage or improve each of these important areas. For each strengths, think "How can we make this strength even stronger?" For weaknesses, try to come up with ways to reduce shortcomings, or turn weaknesses into strengths. For opportunities, think of ways that opportunities can be harnessed and turned into strength. Finally, think of ways to eliminate threats, or turn them into opportunities. It is best to tap into people from many different departments, such as legal, finance, human resources and marketing so that the broadest range of considerations is made when brainstorming. Experts from each area will also know how to best implement plans to take advantage of the SWOT results.

5- Use the results of the SWOT session to guide strategic decisions in the business. Over time SWOT results will change as the business environment changes, so it can be useful to hold new brainstorming sessions on a regular basis.

How to use SWOT Analysis results?

1- Form your planning team. The team should include key members of your operating staff and represent a diverse section of your company.

2- Consider conducting a smaller SWOT analysis on a specific aspect of the business to prime your team for the SWOT evaluation that is company-wide.

3- Set meeting times. Make sure you schedule plenty of time for the team to look over the SWOT analysis. Planning these meetings for the same time each week will help ensure everyone gets into the routine. Although you could also plan a weekend retreat, spreading the meetings out may help your staff generate new ideas and not get stuck in a rut.

4- Make sure everyone is on the same page. Your staff should have trust in each other that their ideas will be respected. Each member should also have the desire to make changes to the company.

5- Define goals for the evaluation at the first meeting. Once everyone has a chance to look over the SWOT analysis, definitive goals should be set. For example, "create three new procedures to ensure customer satisfaction" is a more tangible goal than "plan to increase customer satisfaction."

6- Look over the analysis. See if any line items can fit into multiple categories. For example, a threat of a competitor opening up shop across the street could be an opportunity to solidify your standing in the community by providing exemplary service.

7- Collect data. Although a strength of your business may be your ability to effectively sell to a minority group, that strength will become a weakness if statistics demonstrate a negative growth of the minority group in your community.

8- Decide what you need to improve on. Make a list of all of these goals, and then create a SMART objective for each one.

Make SMART Objectives: Know that SMART stands for specific, measurable, achievable, realistic and time-bound.

9- Define specific objectives. You will need to have objectives with tangible results. One goal may have several objectives---for example, improving your customer service may include performing an annual survey, conducting monthly staff meetings on improving service and hiring more friendly candidates.

10- Decide what you will use to measure your objective. Without standards, there will be no way of demonstrating success or failure of each objective.

11- Brainstorm whether the objective is achievable and how it will be achieved. If your objective is to conduct monthly staff meetings on customer service, then it would be achievable if an appropriate trainer were identified and if time and wages could be allocated to the project.

12- Put some realism into it. Your team will need to really look at each objective to determine if it is realistic. Monthly staff meetings may not seem like a big deal in the meeting room, but coming up with a time that everyone can meet may be.

13- Come up with a timeline. Objectives should be time-bound with start and end dates.

14- Rewrite each objective to take into consideration all of the SMART components. For example, the goal of improving customer service will be transformed into the SMART objective of "Hire a consultant to conduct a staff-wide training on customer service on the first Sunday of each month from January to November of 2010."

Notes*(Place Your Notes Here)*

3- How to setup your project initiation

Project initiation is a very important and articulated phase of the project because it will affect radically the rest of project phases and processes, therefore below are 5 steps to setup your project initiation correctly and safely:-

1- **Review project charter and statement of work:** make sure you have put all stakeholder and your team members on the same page from day one by sharing project charter and statement of work and start getting and recording ideas, risks, recommended approaches and even suggestions to how we should deliver the project? Either one phase or multiple phases to keep client on touch and avoid business requirements changes while we are still developing.

2- **Secure Budget:** no project with no risk, so go spend time identifying risks and build contingency plan and fallback plan if available and accordingly ask for 20-25% extra on the baseline budget if you can get it through higher management and you sponsor.

3- **Get dedicated highly interested sponsor:** go and get that person or authority, you need a dedicated interested person who will support you through the project because he needs the project to succeed just like you or even more, this person will help you while facing challenges, resolving issues and mitigating risks. Make sure that you are strengthening your relationship with that person every day and on.

4- **Setup a steering committee:** having steering committee will eliminate personal agenda from any stakeholders and increase the buy in from different project stakeholders.

5- **Hold the kick-off meeting:** with that step you are putting everybody on the same page and announcing the start of the project will give the team members green light to start their activities and submitting their timesheets which is very important practice to have from day one in your project.

Notes*(Place Your Notes Here)*

4- How to create an effective project charter

One of the most critical document in the Project Life Cycle is the Project Charter. Without this, your project is same as a ship without a rudder. You have nothing to guide you in the precise direction.

The Project Charter identifies the project vision, targets, range, organization and execution plan. It helps you to fix the direction for the project and get buy in from your stakeholders as to how the project will be prepared and accomplished. It will also assist you to control the scope of your project, by determining precisely what it is that you have to attain. Below are the necessary elements for effective project charter:-

1- **Know the Project Vision:** The first measure taken when determining a Project Charter is to identify the project vision. The vision encapsulates the purpose of the project and is the fixed end goal for the project team.
    - Identify your objectives. Then supported on the vision, list three to 5 targets to be reached by the project. Every aim should be Proper, Great, Attainable, Real and Time-bound (SMART).
    - Determine the Scope. With a good prospect of the Vision and Targets of the project, it's time to determine the project scope. The scope specifies the prescribed edges of the project by identifying how the business will be changed or altered by the project delivery.

2- **Describe the Project System:** The succeeding step is to identify how the project will be structured by listing the clients, stakeholders, functions, responsibilities and reporting lines.
    - **Customers**: First, determine the project customers. A client is a person or individual that is obligated for receiving the deliverables when the project is accomplished.

- **Stakeholders:** Then determine the project stakeholders. A stakeholder is a person or entity within or outside of the project with a specific key involvement or stake in the project. For example, a Financial Controller will be involved in the price of the project, and a CEO will be concerned in whether the project aids to attain the company vision.
- **Roles**: Now list the main roles needed in delivering the project. Examples of roles specifies the Project Sponsor, Project Board and Project Manager. Then sum up each of the serious obligations of each role known.
- **Structure**: Once you get a good survey of the functions essential to undertake the project, you can describe the reporting lines between those purposes within a Project Organization Chart.

3- **Arrange the Approach to Implementation**: You now have a solid definition of what the project requires to accomplish and how it will be arranged to accomplish it. The succeeding step is to distinguish the implementation approach as follows.
- **Implementation Plan**: To give the Client and Stakeholders with confidence that the project execution has been well thought through, create an Implementation Plan naming the phases, activities and timeframes required in undertaking the project.
- **Milestones:** In addition, list several necessary milestones and describe why they are vital to the project. A milestone is typically an important project event, such as the achievement of a key deliverable.
- **Dependencies**: Name some key dependencies and their criticality to the project. A dependency is defined as an action that is probably to impact on the project during its life cycle.
- **Resource Plan**: Develop a plan which sums up the funds included in undertaking the project by listing the labor, equipment and materials involved. Then budget the financial resources needed.

4- **List the Dangers and Troubles**: The last step needed to complete your Project Charter is to specify some project dangers, issues, premises and constraints related to the project.

Notes(Place Your Notes Here)

```
┌─────────────────────────────────────────────────────────┐
│                                                         │
│                                                         │
│                                                         │
└─────────────────────────────────────────────────────────┘
```

5- How to build an effective team

There are not big secrets to successful effective teams. Effective team is not about mastering sophisticated theories but rather using a common sense consistently in you interaction with you team members. We have 5 characteristics for effective team:-

- **Clear Purpose and Expectations:** the project manager plays a main role in forming the team by ensuring that all team members have a shared understanding of:-
    a. How their project fits in the overall strategic plans and directions of the organization.
    b. What actions they need to take to reach the defined goals.
    c. How they will be measured along the way.
    d. Project Scope.
- **Trust:** is the foundation of any high performing team. It must be earned and when lost it is impossible to restore. Trust is built when team members know that they can rely on each other to do what they say they will do. Trust grows when team members :-
    a. Respect commitments to deliver quality work on schedule.
    b. Maintain Confidence.
    c. Treat other that way you want to be treated with dignity and respect.
- **Clearly Defined Roles:** Team members must have clearly defined roles and understanding their individual responsibilities at different stages in the project.
    a. **Required Skills**: It is the responsibility of the project manager to identify the mix of the skills required to complete the project and if there are gaps in competencies the project manager has to fill those gaps using available resources because schedules, quality and

project manager's reputation are affected when the team does not have the required skills to do the job.

   b. **Set Expectations**: Once the team is identified it is the project manager responsibility to let every team member know his deliverables, schedule and dependencies.
   c. **Balancing**: One more challenge for the project manager which is balancing between matrix structured team members who reports to project manager and functional manager. Project manager must resolve any conflict raises because of dual reporting.
   d. **RACI**: this document must be created and tied with the project scope, since roles vary during the project you have to encourage flexibility in team members' attitude.
- **Accountable for results:** effective teams have leaders and team members who hold themselves and their peers accountable for results and behavior which means that each team member is responsible for what he delivers and how he interacts inside and outside the team and committed to what he has to deliver on time.
- **Clear, honest and Open Communications:** successful teams communicate effectively and frequently as needed with each other due to communication plan or RACI document, also consistently outside and inside the project team. Encourage team members to tell you the status regardless it is good or bad clearly without any cosmetics.

Notes(Place Your Notes Here)

6- How to conduct effective kickoff meeting

The kickoff meeting for a new project is your best opportunity to energize the group and establish a common purpose toward completing the work. A great kickoff is the result of good planning. After you've done your project preparation work, you need to plan for an effective meeting. Below are developed set of tactics you should use to set the tone for the meeting. They will help you stay organized, establish your leadership, and begin molding the individual project participants into a team. These tips should help you lead more productive project kickoff meetings.

The agenda: As in any effective meeting, participants are better off when they have a clear understanding of how it will progress. Agenda should be simple and contain

- Purpose
- Goals and Deliverables
- Project members Introduction and their roles
- Project assumptions
- High level project plan (Phases)
- Key Success Factors
- Status meeting strategy
- Other Communication Plans
- Questions and answers
- Summary

The meeting: Keep the meeting flowing and avoid wasting time. Be personable and have fun; everyone will enjoy participating more if you take this approach.

Getting started: Take immediate charge of the meeting. Welcome all participants and don't forget to introduce yourself. Briefly explain that you'll walk everyone through the agenda and material and that you'll leave time for questions at the end.

Define the project, its purpose, and expected goals and deliverables. Introduce the project members and briefly discuss the role of each. You should do most of the talking in this first meeting. The kickoff is intended to bring everyone up to speed, not to discuss every item in detail. Every participant needs to see you taking charge of the meeting agenda.

Presenting the project: Now that you've set the tone, discuss the project assumptions that set the stage for how you developed the plan. Refer to the project plan document you sent to everyone and ask them to go through it task by task. Explain and reinforce to everyone that this is a "first cut" and that the important thing to do is verify that the tasks are comprehensive, assigned appropriately, and have reasonable time frames. The time to modify the plan is before the next meeting. Explain that the project plan becomes the foundation for status meetings and is used as the primary communication vehicle for managing the project.

Refer to the tasks that are potential bottlenecks in completing the project. Keep your discussion to the point. Don't get bogged down, but take the opportunity to help staff members anticipate problems. Reinforce key success factors and explain why they are important.

Establish a timeline and team member expectations: Determine an appropriate time and day of the week to conduct weekly one-hour project status meetings. Reinforce the need for everyone to attend and to have that week's tasks completed.

Take time to remind the group that teamwork is essential. Reinforce the need for participants to look out for one another. The objective is to complete the project successfully, and it is up to everyone to do their part and to help one another.

Empower team members to own their responsibilities and to ask for help. Repeat that you expect everyone to attend project status meetings prepared and with all tasks completed, unless you know well ahead of time that there are obstacles. Part of your project management job is to help the team identify bottlenecks and to eliminate obstacles.

Explain the communication plan: Discuss your plan to share information and updates with the group and interested parties, including the following:

- Weekly project status meetings
- Subproject planning sessions
- Project plan status updates
- Senior management updates
- Use of the company intranet or other communication vehicles

Emphasize the need to communicate anything that team members see that might affect the project.

Ask for feedback and then close: Open up the meeting for questions and answers. Be certain you've blocked out ample time. If time runs out, ask everyone to send questions to you or to call you. You can later send out an FAQ or even post it on your company intranet for people interested in staying abreast of the project.

Summarize the meeting with a call for action and list outstanding items that require immediate follow-up. Provide direction on any follow-up communication needed and what you expect from everyone at the first project status meeting.

Notes*(Place Your Notes Here)*

Project Planning

The Project Planning Phase is the second phase in the project life cycle. It involves creating of a set of plans to help guide your team through the execution and closure phases of the project.

The plans created during this phase will help you to manage time, cost, quality, change, risk and issues. They will also help you manage staff and external suppliers, to ensure that you deliver the project on time and within budget.

The Project Planning Phase is often the most challenging phase for a Project Manager, as you need to make an educated guess of the staff, resources and equipment needed to complete your project. You may also need to plan your communications and procurement activities, as well as contract any 3rd party suppliers.

1- How to perform stakeholder analysis

What Is Stakeholder Analysis? A "stakeholder" can be defined as:

"Any individual, group, or institution who has a vested interest in the natural resources of the project area and/or who potentially will be affected by project activities and have something to gain or lose if conditions change or stay the same."

Stakeholders are all those who need to be considered in achieving project goals and whose participation and support are crucial to its success. Stakeholder analysis identifies all primary and secondary stakeholders who have a vested interest in the issues with which the project or policy is concerned. The goal of stakeholder analysis is to develop a strategic view of the human and institutional landscape, and the relationships between the different stakeholders and the issues they care about most.

Why Stakeholder Analysis Is Important? Ultimately, all projects depend on selecting stakeholders with whom they can jointly work towards goals that will reduce or reverse the threats to your key conservation targets.

A stakeholder analysis can help in identifying:

- The interests of all stakeholders who may affect or be affected by the project.

- Potential conflicts or risks that could jeopardize the initiative.

- Opportunities and relationships that can be built on during implementation.

- Groups that should be encouraged to participate in different stages of the project.

- Appropriate strategies and approaches for stakeholder engagement.
- Ways to reduce negative impacts on vulnerable and disadvantaged groups.

The full participation of stakeholders in both project design and implementation of is a key to – but not a guarantee of – success. Stakeholder participation:

- Gives people some say over how projects or policies may affect their lives.
- Is essential for sustainability.
- Generates a sense of ownership if initiated early in the development process.
- Provides opportunities for learning for both the project team and stakeholders themselves.
- Builds capacity and enhances responsibility.

How to Perform Stakeholder Analysis?

Step 1: Identification of key stakeholders: In identifying the key stakeholders, you should consider the following questions:

- Who are the potential beneficiaries?
- Who might be adversely Impacted?
- Have vulnerable groups who may be impacted by the project been identified?
- Have supporters and opponents of the project been identified?
- What are the relationships among the stakeholders?

Answering these questions will lead to a simple list, which forms the basis of the stakeholder analysis

Step 2: Assess stakeholder interests and the potential impact of the project on these interests: Once the key stakeholders have been identified, the possible interest that these groups or individuals may have in the project can be considered.

Questions that you should try to answer in order to assess the interests of different stakeholders include:

- What are the stakeholder's expectations of the project?
- What benefits are likely to result from the project for the stakeholders?
- What resources might the stakeholders be able and willing to mobilize?
- What stakeholder interests conflict with project goals?

Important to realize when assessing the interests of the different stakeholders is that some stakeholders may have hidden, multiple or contradictory aims and interests.

Step 3: Assessing stakeholder influence (Power) and importance (Interest): In the third step the task is to assess the influence and importance of the stakeholders that you identified in earlier steps. Influence refers to the power that the stakeholders have over a project. This power may be in the form of stakeholders that have formal control over the decision-making process of it can be informal in the sense of hindering or facilitating the project's implementation. Importance relates to the question how important the active involvement of the stakeholder is for achievement of the project objectives. Stakeholders who are important are often stakeholders who are to benefit from the project or whose objectives converge with the objectives of the project. You should realize that some stakeholders who are very important might have very little influence and vice versa

In order to assess the importance and influence of the stakeholder you should be able to assess:

- The power and status (political, social and economic) of the stakeholder.
- The degree of organization of the stakeholder.
- The control the stakeholder has over strategic resources.
- The informal influence of the stakeholder (personal connections, etc.).
- The importance of these stakeholders to the success of the project.

Both the influence and importance of the different stakeholders can be ranked along simple scales and mapped against each other. This exercise is an initial step in determining the appropriate strategy for the involvement of these stakeholders. As with the second step, in order to make sure the assessment is as accurate as possible it would be preferable to have 'on the-ground' consultations.

Step 4: Outline a participation strategy: On the basis of the previous three steps in the stakeholder analysis process, some preliminary planning can be done in relation to the question of how to best involve the different stakeholders. The involvement of stakeholders should be planned according to:

- Interests, importance, and influence of each stakeholder.
- Particular efforts needed to involve important stakeholders who lack influence.
- Appropriate forms of participation throughout the project cycle.

As a rule of thumb, the appropriate approaches for involving stakeholders of differing levels of influence and importance can be as follows:

- **Stakeholders of high influence and high importance (Manage Closely):** should be closely involved throughout the preparation and implementation of the project to ensure their support for the project.

- **Stakeholders of high influence but low importance (Keep Satisfied):** are not the target of the project but could possibly oppose the project that you propose. Therefore, you would want to keep them informed and acknowledge their views on the project in order to avoid disruption or hindrance of the project's preparation and implementation.

- **Stakeholders of low influence and high importance (Keep Informed):** require special efforts to ensure that their needs are met and that their participation is meaningful.

- **Stakeholders of low influence and low importance (Monitor – Minimum Effort):** are unlikely to be closely involved in the project and require no special participation strategies (beyond information-sharing to the general public).

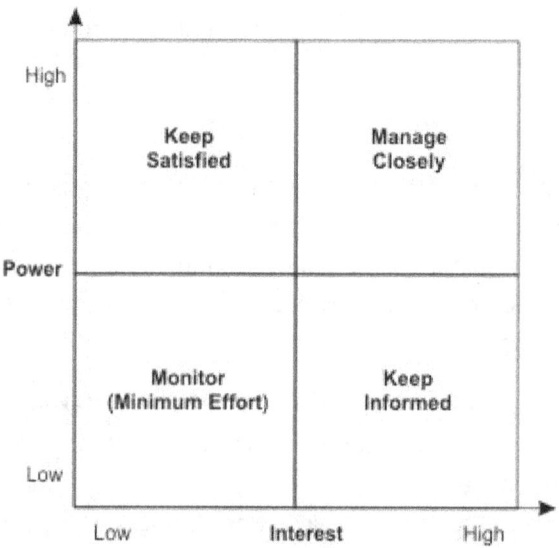

Power / Interest Grid for Stakeholder Prioritization

Notes *(Place Your Notes Here)*

2- How to manage a high risk project

First of all risk is not always something bad, it might be a threat you need to mitigate or avoid or an opportunity to you need to gain, some project managers always try to get away from high risk projects. I can assure that they lost the whole experience and excitement because people get learned from issues they are facing throughout the project but to gain experience and gain success in the same time you need to do the following:-

1- **Plot and manage risk:** from day one go and identify your risks and use everybody in your team, project stakeholders and even your company risk experts then develop your strategy and mitigation plans and do not leave the plans on the papers and shelves but assign someone capable enough for following up and executing those plans and leverage all needed help and support he might need during execution. One last thing do not leave the action owner and go away but go and see it yourself and follow up with him on plan execution progress.

2- **Divide the project into small versions:** as much as you can try to divide your project into small versions (iterations or phases) where you can measure the progress and client can feel the benefit of the version to his business and his organization, in this way you ensure that every step you are taking in the right track and even if client decided to roll back soit will be one step (version), not big work where you will not be able to recover or burry it in the whole project budget. In each version go a study the risks again do not depend on the first identification because even provided versions from your side might affect the initial risk assessment you already did.

3- **Get star team:** high risk project needs a talent team to take over, so try to get star team members as much as you can and if you found a team member who is not giving the project the needed attention or he is giving negative attitude or impressions all the time go and speak to him either to stick with the team spirit or get out of the project because his existence in the project will harm you more than leaving it.

4- **Stakeholder management:** it is the most important point, you must be very honest and transparent in communications with project stakeholders. If you have bad news go and study for solutions and convey it them very honestly and transparently, In this way you bring them in your side to support and help you to recover the issues because it is their project and success before it is yours. One last thing is to build your relationships with them because you will need those relationships later in the project to get their support or their authority or other teams you might have dependencies on them.

Finally, you will be a star only when you do something exceptional like managing and delivering a high risk project so do not hesitate to handle it, do not hesitate to be rewarded.

Notes(Place Your Notes Here)

3- How to estimate more accurately

Estimating activity duration accurately is important to the success of any project. You and your team estimate the various requirements of cost, time, and resources throughout your project. Although activity duration estimation looks at the time it takes to complete the entire project, activity duration estimation is dependent on other time and resource estimates.

You might start on these estimates at the inception of the project, but you make the most of the estimates during the planning phase. It's a good idea that all the people who implement the plan participate in preparing it.

Estimates are never exact. That's their nature — they are best guesses. But you can improve your accuracy by dividing the estimation task into three distinct steps: determining a Work Breakdown Structure (WBS), estimating the amount of work and duration of work packages, and calculating the project schedule.

1- **Determine the Work Breakdown Structure (WBS)**: The Work Breakdown Structure (WBS) is an estimating tool that defines a project in terms of its deliverables. The WBS also provides a method for breaking down deliverables into meaningful units of work. With this breakdown, you establish the work hierarchy and create a foundation for the other elements of the estimating process.

   A WBS is divided into work levels. Work packages are at the lowest levels (or "end nodes") of each branch of your WBS. A work package usually refers to a unit of work to be performed within your organization.

Get your stakeholders involved when you start on your WBS. They can provide information on tasks and resources that might otherwise be overlooked. Generally, the more complete your WBS, the more accurate your duration estimate.

When creating your WBS:

a. Develop your WBS before scheduling or allocating resources.

b. Do not use your WBS to show the work sequence.

c. Involve knowledgeable individuals in your WBS development.

d. Break down your project only as far as you must for accurate estimation.

e. Do not force all paths on your WBS down to the same level.

f. Use no more than 20 levels.

2- **Estimate the duration of work packages**: The duration of a work package is equal to the amount of time required to do the work, divided by the number of people working (duration=work/number of people).

After you have the raw estimate for a work package, you need to add some padding to get a realistic number. The padding accounts for real-life factors such as:

- **Lost time** Team members and workers are not available five days per week, 52 weeks per year. Personal or public holidays, sickness, training, group meetings, family emergencies, and other events affect the time that workers can spend on the job. Keep these factors in mind when you calculate the duration of work packages. You can use enterprise calendars in project-tracking systems, such as Microsoft Office Project Professional 2003, to help you make accurate estimates that allow for these time losses.

- **Part-time work** Assigning part-time work on a given work package lengthens its duration. Half-time work doubles the duration, three-quarter work adds 50% to the duration, and so on. Consult personal schedules and work hours when calculating the effect of part-time work on your estimate.
- **Interference** Physical constraints or features of the work location can have a negative impact on effectiveness and increase work package duration. Areas with limited access or workspace might cause workers to get in each other's way or limit their use of facilities. For instance, in a room that accommodates only one worker at a time, adding another worker does not decrease duration, but might add to it instead. Fax machines, phones, noise, proximity of machinery, placement of equipment, and even traffic flow might cause interference. As interference rises, productivity falls and work duration rises. Take into account the possible interference factor when you make your duration estimate.
- **Communication** Communication takes time. While communication is good, trying to communicate too much between too many team members can increase work duration. The number of communication channels grows exponentially as the number of team members increases. Messages can also lag when distance and time-zone differences are involved. Include the communication factor in your estimate.

Experience and the use of historical data also improves your estimates. If you've done a task frequently — or have a lot of documentation for similar tasks — you'll know the task's average duration. After you know the level of human resources available to do the work, you can use this average in calculating your estimate. But because estimates are not exact, an average duration is only that — an average. In practice, the duration has a 50% chance of being higher or lower than the average.

With this in mind, it's tempting to pad your estimate a lot and increase the probability that the work is completed on time or ahead of time. But beware: Pad with care. Over padding increases budget costs. If your budget is too fat, your project might not get funded.

Some projects don't lend themselves well to standard estimating techniques. Historical data becomes particularly useful in these cases. For instance, most software projects are not mechanistic and activities can be indeterminate, so estimating project duration for software development has always been difficult. But by tailoring their model to their needs and using historical data about similar projects, many software companies produce better estimates than ever before. Using historical data provides a key to better estimation.

3- **Calculate the project schedule**: When your WBS is complete and you have duration estimates for all the work packages, you and your project team can determine the overall project duration. The two most common estimating methods for this are the Critical Path Method (CPM) and the Performance Evaluation Review Technique (PERT).

The differences between CPM and PERT are:

- CPM calculates the total project duration based on individual task durations and their interdependencies. The sequence of tasks determining the minimum time needed for the project is the critical path.
- PERT is a pictorial description of project tasks as a network of dependencies. Although it is also concerned with critical paths, PERT looks at the most likely time estimates for tasks and boundary times (time windows) for tasks.

Next, you need to know the early start and finish dates, the late start and finish dates, and the float. Calculate the early start and finish dates by using software which is very commonly used nowadays.

When you've identified the early start and finish dates, the late start and finish dates, and the float, you and your project team can identify the critical path. The critical path is the shortest path on the project. If a task on the critical path is delayed, the entire project is delayed.

With all this information assembled, you can calculate your schedule and complete your estimate of project duration.

Final estimate: A structured and disciplined approach to estimating project duration helps you create a comprehensive estimate that reflects real tasks and real-world scheduling. This approach removes uncertainty and creates a project plan that helps you know your options and adapt to path changes. Sound duration estimation also supports realistic budget estimates that increase your project's chance of success. Even though estimates are never exact, solid data and good estimating practices make your "best guesses" better.

Notes*(Place Your Notes Here)*

4- How to plot project risks

If you think as a project manager that you can identify and handle all projects' risks, you are wrong. No one can see the full picture in details and find all risks face the project, so in order to effectively plot your project risks follow these actions:-

1- **Get all risks list:** gather you team members, senior management- or at least representative- and your client stakeholders –or at least a representative- and give sticky notes colored where each color represent project area like (Cost, Quality, time and budget) then ask them to write as much as they can all risks they see on the project respecting the color methodology. Once they finished take all inputs and filter them and push it into "Risk Register".
2- **Set Probability and Impact:** have a team with relevant team members who has experience in such field or with riskexperience if you have one in your organization to set the probability(likelihood) and impact of each risk, do not go in details make it simple and short rating like (High, Medium and Low).
3- **Develop mitigation techniques:** identify the high priority risks calculated from 2nd action and start developer proper mitigation techniques for each risk which can be
    a. **For Opportunities**
        i. **Exploit:** where the plan or / and scope might change to ensure getting the opportunity(most of the time this technique is costly)
        ii. **Enhance:** where you do actions to enhance your status to increase the probability of getting the opportunity.
        iii. **Share:** hiring third party to share the opportunity with you so both of you get the benefit.

iv. **Accept:** no further actions to get the opportunity but studying and waiting for that opportunity.
   b. **For Risks**
      i. **Avoid:** where the plan or / and scope might change to avoid the risk totally (most of the time this technique is costly)
      ii. **Mitigate:** where you do actions to reduce the impact of the risk to an accepted limit (which will follow the organization risk tolerance)
      iii. **Transfer:** hiring third party to take actions to reduce the risk and take the full responsibility when risks happen.
      iv. **Accept:** no further actions to get the risk but studying and waiting for that risk.
4- **Quantify Mitigation and Impact:** in order to get approval for mitigation technique you have to transfer it into dollars language which senior management can understand, because the total amount of quantifying the mitigation will be the contingency amount you can ask from management.

Finally, risk identification is not something to be done once in the project, above actions must be repeated at least weekly to make sure that risks assessment remained the same and so your mitigations techniques.

Notes(Place Your Notes Here)

5- How to include risk factor into your estimations

Risk is a constant struggle for many project managers. Many know that risks are important but they do not always know where to find them, list them, or account for them. Risk is an important factor when talking about estimations, especially when it is calculated using PERT Method.

PERT Method: a method to analyze the involved tasks in completing a given project, especially the time needed to complete each task, and to identify the minimum time needed to complete the total project.

PERT Formula: [(Best Scenario Est.) + 4* (Most Likely Est.) + (Worst Scenario Est.)] / 6

Now, the question is: "What makes that your worst case estimate?" Answers could be, "This is a new technology that we have never worked with," or, "The team is geographically dispersed so communication may not be as fast." This type of information will become the basis of when to add risk and when not to.

To further qualify when to add risk or not, let's first understand why this is a consideration. Although risk is accounted for in the PERT formula, there are two types. There is the risk that the team member has simply underestimated the length of the task. There is also the risk that an outside influence could cause the delay. Delineating which risk is which is why the question, "What makes it your worst case?" should be asked.

If the team member states that he is just unsure of how long the task will take, then he or she is adding a buffer. These risks are time risks, and the PERT formula should account for this. Some tasks will finish early, and some will finish late. PERT will assist in accounting for both types.

If the team member states that there is an outside influence, then PERT is generally not handling that risk. For example, if the resource said, "I think

15 days is my worst-case scenario because the part we needis unavailable." This situation constitutes a risk that should be identifiedand accounted for in addition to PERT. PERT is a fantastic tool to helpaccount for the unknowns in a project and a way to identify critical pathtasks. It is also a great way to ask resources to think of everything thatcan occur and capture risks. In asking your team members to quantify thetime estimates, they begin to explain why they have added time to the estimate.

The project manager now can list the risks that are a result of roadblocks, issues,or outside influences. This list also allows the project manager to judge the comfortlevel of each resource in their estimates. Communication being key,this is a great exercise for a PM to perform with his or her team.

Notes(Place Your Notes Here)

6- How to plan/manage project quality

Before getting into actions how to manage quality in your project let us make sure that word "quality" is clear for you:

What is Quality? Quality is some targets you and stakeholders are putting together in the beginning of the project / phase so during executing you are making sure you are working to meet these targets.

So quality is something unique, it is totally different from project to another and from product to another, that is why you have to keep in mind "Quality is planned and not inspected", meaning do not wait until testing phase to come then inspect the quality of the product.

To make things more clear, we have three stages:-

1- **Quality Planning**: as we described above which is to set the targets, policies and procedures.
2- **Quality Assurance:** is to make sure that project is following the policies and procedure set in the planning phase.
3- **Quality Control:** is to inspect the product to make sure it meets the targets set in the planning phase.

Here are actions to manage quality better in your project:-

1- **Define Quality:** go and **discuss** with your project stakeholders and **agree** on quality targets headlines, policies, procedures and if needed third party to ensure the quality.

2- **Set Targets:** after setting the vision or headlines you have to literally set deterministic targets which can be measured later on, keep these targets clear where no one might have any misunderstanding later on.

3- **Communicate Target:** decide who will communicate, monitor and maintain those targets in the sub plans and identify who is going to test those targets and approve the results.

4- **Measure Targets:** keep your eyes on the results and make sure that you are meeting your targets metrics with the accepted tolerance level.

5- **Take Actions:** if you found any deviation which is not accepted by the quality limits defined in the planning phase, you must take an action either by escalating the issue, cancel the project if it is sever deviation or going step back and study what is happing, sometimes last action is better than insisting on resolving the issues.

Notes(Place Your Notes Here)

7- How to select outsourcing vendor effectively

The process of selecting an outsourcing vendor implies a complex multistage process to evaluate not only what the provider can do, but also the way it's done.

First of all it's important know that this process can and should take some time. Sometimes, this means months. A well-organized vendor selection usually takes between 6 and 12 months and can ramp up the total cost of the project with approx. 1-10%. Costs associated with this phase include analysis and documentation of requirements; creation, distribution and evaluation of RFPs (Request for Proposals); negotiations of contracts; development of SLAs (service level agreements); pay of external players: consultants, lawyers etc.

Therefore, the selection of vendor is not a process to be rushed. Companies should follow a well-established methodology that defines each step of the trip. After all, the final goal is to end up with the best service provider for delivering the desired outcome.

1- **Define your objectives and goals:** This is a basic step for all future outsourcing activities. You have to describe the process, service or product that you want outsourced clearly. You should also indicate what your goals are through outsourcing.

   Another one of the first things you should do is gather a core team to evaluate vendors and participate in negotiations. The team should consist of individuals from various parts of the company, such as executives from affected business departments, legal staff and human resources responsible.

   Make sure you include the answer to the following questions in formulating your objectives:

   - What do you want to outsource?
   - What type of an outsourcing agreement are you looking for?

- What are the offshore outsourcing locations that you are interested in?
- What are your goals in outsourcing?
- What services do you expect a vendor to provide?
- How much do you plan to spend?
- What are the risks associated with such an outsourcing agreement?

The team's first task should be to define the high-level requirements of the outsourcing engagement. For instance, if the goal for outsourcing is to reduce costs, the organization should state it openly and leverage this process to explore ways to achieve that goal. The next step is to benchmark the current process against others in the industry. Drawing "before" and "after" process maps is a great exercise that helps companies explain where they are today and show where they want the outsourcer to take them.

Next, it's critical that the core team determines the right type of services to be outsourced. There are many different kinds of work outsourced. However all of these outsourcing services fall in two broad categories, **technology services outsourcing** and **business process outsourcing**.

2- **Find out all you need to know about the vendor – Plan the RFI**: The Request for Information (RFI) provides material for the first rounds of vendor evaluations. Organizations generally use the RFI to validate vendor interest and to evaluate the business climate in the organization's industry. As opposed to a highly specific, formal Request for Proposal (RFP), the RFI encourages vendors to respond freely. It also spells out the business requirements defined by the core team, so the vendor understands what the company is trying to accomplish.
- A request for information is just that – requesting information
- It is usually issued to acquire information on what is available, from whom and what approximate cost before writing an RFP that is based on real information rather than wishful thinking.

- Typically, vendors will not respond to an RFI unless the effort to do so is not excessive and there is an expectation that an order or at least an RFP will follow.

Contents of RFI: The type of information usually sought by RFI's includes things such as:

- The availability of equipment or needed services.
- The approximate one time and recurring costs.
- The differentiating factors between the goods or services proposed and similar offerings from other vendors.

The latter is very useful in providing information to help determine mandatory and desirable characteristics to be included in an RFP.

After vendors return the questionnaire, the issuing company matches the vendors' responses to the company's requirements and weights the criteria based on importance. Providers that don't meet stated needs or haven't responded to the specific questions are eliminated.

Eventually, the RFI process helps companies make the "go or no go" decision—that is, the choice to proceed with or walk away from a project. The data solicited identifies the availability and viability of outsourcing, cost estimate ranges, and risks. It also provides detail useful for developing project requirements.

3- **Prepare the RFP:** The third step is to develop the RFP; send it to at least three short-listed suppliers; evaluate them; and, of course, select the best ones.

The RFI and RFP are complementary. Information collected during the RFI process can prepare the solution requirements section of the related RFP. You should have by now a better understanding of project scope and requirements, as well as a list of qualified suppliers. Leveraging the information-gathering focus of the RFI will lead to a concise RFP that articulates the business needs.

The RFP outlines the engagement's requirements—relevant skill sets, language skills, intellectual property protection, infrastructure, and quality certifications—and gives prospective vendors the information necessary to prepare a bid. The responsibility of developing the RFP rests with the project's sourcing leader, but various aspects of the document will require input from other domain experts.

A good RFP includes one section that states what the company seeks (business requirements) and four sections that ask about the vendor and what it will be able to provide:

- **Business requirements**: In brief, this section details the company's project goal, deliverables, performance and fulfillment requirements, and liquidity damages.
- **Vendor profile**: External service providers differ greatly in performance, style, and experience. This part of the RFP details the vendor's stability, services, and reputation.
- **Vendor employee information:** This section addresses the resources assigned at the project management, middle management, team leader, and task levels, along with the quality of people, their skills, training, compensation, and retention. If your company ranks technical skills highest should look at technical expertise before examining costs.
- **Vendor methodology**: The methodology segment details project management, quality, regulatory compliance and security.
- **Infrastructure**: This part outlines the vendor's infrastructure stability and disaster-recovery abilities.

4- **Due Diligence:** After vendors have sent their RFP responses, you begin the evaluation.

Usually, vendors propose different strategies when they respond to an RFP. They may suggest a sole provider, co sourcing, or multi-sourcing scenario, in which one, two, or several vendors, respectively, deliver the service to the company. Regardless of the structure, if the proposal meets the stated requirements, each vendor must then undergo a due diligence review.

Due diligence supports or invalidates the information the vendor supplied on processes, financials, experience and performance. It helps you determine what the provider can do right now, as opposed to what it might do if given the business. Due diligence should confirm the information supplied in the RFP and address the following data:

- Company profile, strategy, mission and reputation
- Financial status - reviews of audited financial statements
- Customer references - preferably from similar outsourced processes
- Management qualifications, including criminal background checks
- Process expertise, methodology and effectiveness
- Quality initiatives and certifications
- Technology, infrastructure stability and applications
- Security and audit controls
- Legal and regulatory compliance, including any outstanding complaints or litigation
- Use of subcontractors
- Insurance
- Disaster recovery, security and business continuity policies

Pay attention also to employee policies, attrition, service attitudes and management values; the company and the vendor need to fit together culturally.

You should evaluate the vendor's project management competency, the level of success achieved, the quality and standards of work delivered, adherence to contract terms, and the communication process. Reliable, ongoing communications, especially in offshore outsourcing is very important; potential pitfalls can result from infrequent or vague communications. For instance, if the onshore company doesn't clearly communicate deliverables andtimelines, offshore resources might not be allocated correctly and may endanger completing the project on time.

Sometimes you must perform due diligence on more than one of the vendors that respond. The length and formality of the due diligence process varies according to companies' experience with outsourcing, the timeline for implementing outsourcing, the risk, and familiarity with the vendor.

5- **Test Project (Optional):** Some companies can even conduct test projects to ensure a good fit between the company and the vendor.

These tests allow companies to review the vendor's project management process for efficiency and effectiveness. Specifically, they look at whether project execution is completed within guidelines, whether deliverables are timely and whether the vendor has adhered to defined quality standards. Tests serve as a good method for companies to check and review the facts before making a final vendor decision.

Test projects also let companies experience the benefits of outsourcing before jumping into a long-term relationship. Often, companies will conduct a "proof of concept" (POC) with a couple of vendors to compare results and, after evaluation, choose the best one. A good method to select the best vendor is by taking the top two vendors from the RFP process and having them complete the same test project. This will demonstrate their project management capabilities, communication style, and ability to meet deadlines for deliverables. Many companies are using POCs as test beds before offshoring larger projects.

6- **Choose the Vendor:** Eventually, the biggest step in the process of selection is picking a service provider to manage business processes and applications. Making the final decision means signing a contract that clearly defines the performance measures, team size, team members, pricing policies, business continuity plans and overall quality of work standards

Successful Project Managers Roadmap

Notes*(Place Your Notes Here)*

8- How to avoid common outsourcing pitfalls

1- **Poor Governance:** This is one of the most commonly encountered problems and a key cause of failure of an outsourcing relationship. Organizations often take a tactical approach to outsourcing and do not pay attention to executive sponsorship, which is an important ingredient for success. Lack of a structured governance mechanism has led to the "untimely demise" of several outsourcing relationships.

   A good governance model ensures a strategy which clearly defines the objective of outsourcing, prescribes a working model that is flexible and collaborative, sets up SLAs and decides on a mechanism for arbitrating issues.

   Most outsourcers, however, woefully under invest in the ongoing governance and management of the service provider relationship and this invariably spells trouble for the engagement.

2- **Shortsighted Focus on Cost Savings:** Most enterprises that have outsourced their IT requirements cite cost savings as the key reason for doing so. This often results in raising unrealistic expectations with reference to continual cost savings. Owing to this myopic view, enterprises fail to consider other benefits such as process efficiency, improved focus on core business areas, better ability to plan, higher levels of operational reliability, and more rapid implementation of new strategies and initiatives.

   A broader and long term approach is essential to set pragmatic goals, spread over time for evaluating the success of a relationship. Some of the other benefits enterprises should seek from outsourcing engagements include access to flexible, scalable and easy to maintain systems — leeway to focus on core strategic functions, access to high caliber labour and more importantly riskmitigation. When enterprises broaden their vision and visualize outsourcing as a strategic function, they will be able to adopt a more balanced approach as opposed to viewing it as a pure cost reduction mechanism.

3- **Lack of Preparation - Seeing Outsourcing as an Instant Solution:**
Using outsourcing as a quick fix to alleviate certain immediate problems is yet another commonly encountered issue that leads to poor results. While outsourcing does result in some operational sweet spots, it should not be the primary reason to employ this strategy. This mindset leaves an enterprise under prepared for outsourcing.

Many a times, companies start the request for proposal (RFP) and contract negotiation processes before they have thoroughly evaluated the outsourcing decision internally. Outsourcing being a complex decision, such an unplanned approach will jeopardize the future of the relationship.

To ensure a successful and lasting outsourcing engagement, the organization must prepare itself for the change it will have to undergo during this transformation. Issues such as job loss and resistance to change will crop up during the transition and needs to be guarded against.

4- **Failure toDevelop an Effective Communication Program:**
Communication is a key factor in delivering results in an outsourcing engagement. Sharing of information is essential for :-
- Clarity of expectations and objectives.
- Alignment ofinterests.
- Compatibility between the two parties.

A number of factors such as the distance, time, language, and cultural differences create barriers forcommunication. Also, in cases where cost cutting is the only reason for outsourcing, it has been seenthat communication takes a backseat. For a successful outsourcing relationship, the outsourcer and the service provider need to work in a collaborative manner. Key elements for overcoming barriers forcommunication include:

- Establishing clear communication channels
- Standardized formatfor content,frequency, levels andmodes
- Interactive and proactive communication
- Escalationmechanism
- In global outsourcing relationships,showing diversity

5- **Improper Evaluation of Outsourcing Service Providers:** Often companies invest less time and money on selecting service providers and put the complete project in jeopardy. Proper evaluation and selection of providers is crucial. There are six common mistakes that companies should avoid while evaluating providers :-
- Failure to understand the market
- Time expended on complicated RFPs
- Evaluating too many providers
- Letting service providers take control of the process
- Letting politics cloud decision
- Leaving commercial details to the end.

The pitfalls of choosing the wrong service provider are many. At the minimum it would give sub optimal returns and in the worst case, it may lead to the outsourcer abandoning the engagement. Therefore, It is essential to thoroughly evaluate service providers on their contextual understanding. Before selecting a provider, or even drafting an RFP, it would be a good idea to know the big and up-and-coming providers in that space. This due diligence can come in handy while shortlisting providers.

It is better for a company to stay in control and remain focused on the key criteria, essential for the success of the engagement. Ranking the providers based on certain pre-defined criteria is the best selection method; this also minimizes the subjective influence on the selection.

6- **Poor Cultural Fit – Compatibility of Parties:** At the end of the day, an outsourcing relationship works best when the chemistry between outsourcer and service provider is right. Given that people are at the center of an IT outsourcing arrangement compatibility is essential.

"Cultural Fit is as important as cost saving", the finding is not surprising given that outsourcing is becoming strategic and long term in nature. Consequently, it has become all the more important to find an outsourcer who has similar work ethics, values and ways of doing things.

Businesses are also beginning to see the value in bringing in external consultants to help bridge cultural gaps and iron out differences during negotiations. As a rule, compatibility issues needs to be addressed during the selection process. In addition, effective communication is essential to ensure good cultural fit.

7- **Improper Definition of Metrics and Key Performance Indicators:** Often businesses believe that a set of predefined metrics will help them monitor the performance of the service provider and retain control over the relationship. However, the wrong set of metrics or an overdose of KPIs can do more harm than good to an outsourcing relationship. In the first case, the outsourcer may not get the true picture of whether the relationship is moving in the right direction, and this is dangerous. In the second case, fatigue may defeat the value of the tracking.

Thus, the recommended approach is to choose a few apt metrics that gives the outsourcer a sense of where the engagement is at any point in time. On line dashboards are becoming increasingly common as a means of providing visibility on metrics and KPIs to the buyer.

Finally below List of Do's to help you avoiding above pitfalls:-

1- Make sure that when you start the outsourcing relationship you dedicated the right people and resources on both sides.
2- Make sure your contact persons has very good communication skills.
3- Define as much as possible the expectations, document them, set clear performance metrics and set clear targets.
4- Be prepared for changes; allow flexibility to your contract.
5- Be Prepared for renegotiation the outsourcing the contract one better understands your business.
6- Initiate an agreement with a service provider that allows flexibility for the future.
7- Have a realistic timeline for any steps of the outsource process including the start-up.
8- Fully define an employee transition plan.
9- Do proper planning concerning information systems and interfacing with the service provider.
10- Do enough technology development before implementation.

Notes(Place Your Notes Here)

This page intentionally left blank

Project Execution

The Project Execution Phase is the third phase in the project life cycle. In this phase, you will build the physical project deliverables and present them to your customer for signoff. The Project Execution Phase is usually the longest phase in the project life cycle and it typically consumes the most energy and the most resources.

To enable you to monitor and control the project during this phase, you will need to implement a range of management processes. These processes help you to manage time, cost, quality, change, risks and issues. They also help you to manage procurement, customer acceptance and communications.

1- How to run productive and effective meetings

1- **Purpose:** decide what is the purpose of the meeting what are you trying to accomplish, address or resolve. If you can handle the issue by yourself or with second person then the meeting is not necessary. Run a meeting only if you need inputs from large group of people or there are issues need to be discussed with the participants of the meetings.

2- **Agenda:** if you found this meeting necessary develop and share agenda with the meeting participants at least one week in advance –if possible- the agenda should specify the actions to be discussed and what are outcome expected for each item. The agenda also should specify the time of the meeting and total duration. Sending the agenda enough time in advance help attendees to be prepared to agenda items or ask questions before attending the meeting, also give them enough time to reschedule themselves to the meeting time.

3- **Stick to the agenda:** it is the responsibility of the meeting facilitator to keep all attendees sticking to the agenda items, and if someone tried to get out of the agenda or discuss an issue which is not related to the agenda items he has to hold it and take it to what is called "**Parking Lot**" which means to be discussed at a later stage either in the same meeting or in future meeting.

4- **Time Slot:** facilitator also must allot time slot for each agenda item and make sure that all people stick to it, he can assure this by
    a. Not allowing someone to repeat what someone already said.
    b. Soliciting input from all individuals before letting someone who already spoke to speak again.

5- **Action Items:** before going out of the meeting actions items for each agenda item must be set which include for each action item:
   a. Action to be done.
   b. Who is going to do?
   c. What is the timeframe?

6- **Meeting's Minutes:** which acts like formal message for action items agreed on in the meeting where the facilitator can follow up with team attendees, which gives them more trust in such meetings because they can see the progress.

Notes*(Place Your Notes Here)*

2- How to keep everyone on the same page during the project

Keeping everyone on the same page is very important practice you have to follow during your project life cycle, because missing any stakeholder or isolating any stakeholder is threating your project to be delayed or even be terminated. Here are some actions to keep this practice on:-

1- **Planned Updates:** Using weekly reports and/or weekly meetings where you can state / discuss achieved milestones and planes for next week and detailing any risks / issues / dependencies which might affect next week plans, in this way you are setting everyone expectations about the progress of the project.

2- **Status Report:** It acts like weekly reports but on the whole project stating all key features achieved and plans for next duration, and stating all project risks / issues / dependencies.

3- **Requirements Review Workshop:** Do not keep the requirements on the shelf after writing it by system analyst, bring all key business users together and all relevant stakeholders in a meeting and go through the requirements making sure requirements still valid and as expected when the requirements gathering started.

4- **Design Review Workshop:** There are two types of design which are Technical Design and Business Process Design, again gather all relevant stakeholders and key business users to review the business process or technical design and make sure that business process is still compatible with the requirements.

5- **Test Plans& Scenarios:** Share the test plans with the business users and get their feedback, by having this practice you will make sure that you covered all important scenarios and exceptions that might arise after going live.

6- **User Training before UAT:** Give actual users soft training to the system so they get familiar to the system and how to use it before going into UAT session, in this way you get the first impression comments so you can cover it early enough before UAT sessions.

During all above actions get sign-off and acceptance for each action to protect you throughout the project.

Notes(Place Your Notes Here)

3- How to deliver successful presentation

Any project manager must have presentation skills because he/she will come to the situation of delivering a presentation, to have a successful presentation there are lot of actions and steps you have to take and those actions are divided into 3 parts which are "Before the presentation", "During the presentation" and "After the presentation". Let us take each section and describe how to manage it.

1- **Preparation(Before):**
   a. **Expectations:** In this part you are studying all basic information about your presentation and make sure that is up to what is expected.
      i. **Topic:** make sure that your audience is aware of the topic you are going to talk about.
      ii. **Audience:** know / study your audience because the presentation focus will be different if audience is stakeholders or project team.
      iii. **Location:** select the location properly, make sure that the location will have enough space for all audience, also it must be easily reachable.
      iv. **Venue:** how the presentation will be delivered? Is it conference room or is it conference call?
      v. **Time / Duration:** it is very important to select the proper time for audience, make sure that you selected the time which they will have all the focus on your presentation. Also take care of the duration if it more than 50 minutes divide it into segments and each segment less than 50 minutes.
   b. **Good Research:** it is a key point to have successful presentation, it should be built on good research and not questionable facts.
      i. **Relevancy:** it must be relevant to the audience so they can follow up with you.

ii. **Why do they care?** You have to find an answer to this question so you can emphasize your presentation on this.
iii. **How this can beneficial to them?** If you found this answer you got the audience attention.
c. **Materials:** stay professional and prepare all materials might be needed during the presentation and make sure that you have one focal point where all audience follow up with you like "Power Point".

2- **Presentation (During):** Here we came to the most important section which is the presentation itself, although it is depending so much on your soft presentation skills but here are some tips to have to go through this part successfully
   a. **Arrive & Test:** arrive early enough and test the venue and make sure that everything is properly working.
   b. **Presentation:** that is the main part and as a quick tip on it divide it into 3 main segments
      i. **Intro:** give the audience important fact, statistical or a new idea to get their attentions from the beginning.
      ii. **Message:** detailing the intro to deliver the inner message.
      iii. **Wrap-up:** make sure that you can wrap-up the message in one or two sentences as a follow up on the message.
   c. **Delivery:** how you are presenting is depending on the type of message, like if the message is for inspiration, motivation or it is serious situation. Your tone will be affected by this type. Last note "give space for questions".
   d. **Next Steps:** determine the next steps after the presentation either having another sessions, attending a course or working on proofing the idea you delivered.
   e. **Your Contacts:** mention you contacts details for any further inquiries or questions.

3- **Follow Up (After):** This part is coming after the presentation and it is focusing on the following up on the presentation with the audience.

a. **Send "Thank you":** send a "thank you" mail to the audience for attending your presentation and leave your contacts information.
b. **Follow up on next steps:** try to follow up on next steps and schedule it if it is under your authority and get feedback.

Notes*(Place Your Notes Here)*

4- How to delegate effectively

The secret of success is not in doing your own work, but in recognizing the right person to do it.

One of the most crucial and challenging tasks for managers and supervisors is to apportion the work among the employees they manage and supervise. A lot of managers and supervisors frequently complain that they have too much to do and too little time in which to do it. Unchecked, this feeling leads to stress and ineffectiveness. In many cases, executives could greatly reduce their stress by practicing a critical management skill – delegation.

Delegation is the assignment of authority to another person to carry out the specific job-related activities. It allows a subordinate to make decisions; that is, it is a shift of decision-making authority from one organizational level to another lower one.

Delegation should not be confused with participation. In participative decision making, there is a sharing of authority; with delegation, subordinates make decisions on their own. Effective delegation pushes authority down vertically through the ranks of an organization.

Before describing how to delegate, you have to keep in mind:-

1- **Delegation is not "dumping."**: Managers should take special care to make sure that the employee does not think he is trying to "dump" unpleasant assignments on him.
2- **Delegation is not abdication:** The manager still has the ultimate accountability for the assignment. That's why it is important for you to establish appropriate controls and checkpoints to monitor progress. Besides, managers should give delegates the appropriate authority to act along with clear expectations including any boundaries or criteria. The manager, however,

should try to avoid prescribing HOW the assignment should be completed.

3- **Delegation involves three important concepts and practices**: responsibility, authority, and accountability. When you delegate, you share responsibility and authority with others and you hold them accountable for their performance. The ultimate accountability, however, still lies with the manager who should clearly understand that :

- **Responsibility** refers to the assignment itself and the intended results. That means setting clear expectations. It also means that you should avoid prescribing the employee HOW the assignment should be completed.
- **Authority** refers to the appropriate power given to the individual or group including the right to act and make decisions. It is very important to communicate boundaries and criteria such as budgetary considerations.

- **Accountability** refers to the fact that the relevant individual must 'answer' for his/her/their actions and decisions along with the rewards or penalties that accompany those actions or decisions.

How to delegate?

1- Determine what you are going to delegate. Then take the time to plan how you are going to present the assignment, including your requirements, parameters, authority level, checkpoints and expectations. It is a good idea to write down these items and give a copy to your delegate in order to minimize miscommunication.
2- Choose the right person. Assess the skills and the experience of your employees as objectively as possible. Don't be too quick to choose the person who you always know you can depend on.

3- Give an overview of the assignment including the importance of the assignment and why you have chosen the employee for the job.
4- Describe the new responsibility in detail, outlining sub-tasks, defining any necessary parameters, and setting performance standards. Make sure the employee understands his/her level or degree of authority. Let the employee know who he/she can turn to for help as well as other available resources. By the way, make sure that you notify those affected by the delegates' power.
5- Solicit questions, reactions, and suggestions. At this point you may want to ask the employee what approach he/she might take.
6- Listen to the employee's comments and respond empathetically. This step helps to get employee "buy-in" and will also help you determine if the employee does indeed understand what is expected of him/her.
7- Ask the employee for commitment and offer help or some type of back-up assistance. An employee who already feels overwhelmed may worry about completing the assignments already on his/her plate. It is your responsibility to help establish priorities and relieve some of the pressure by getting someone else to share some of the delegates' routine tasks for the duration of the assignment.
8- Be encouraging. Express confidence in the employee's ability to successfully handle the new responsibility.
9- Establish checkpoints, deadlines, and ways to monitor progress. The entire discussion should be a collaborative process. You should strive for mutual agreement.
10- Keep in contact with the employee and observe the checkpoints the two of you agreed to. However, don't hover. Remember, delegating means letting go.
11- Recognize and reward the person for his/her successful completion of the assignment.

Symptoms of Poor Delegation

There are many symptoms of poor delegation, and can be seen in the working habits of the manager, the attitude of the employees, or the overall productivity of the organization. Check from the following list the symptoms that are visible in your department / organization:

- Deadlines are frequently missed.
- Some employees are much busier than others.
- Competent employees feel frustrated and bored.
- Manager is usually too busy to talk to employees.
- Employees are assigned the tasks with proper training.
- Employees are unsure of their authority and responsibility.
- Employees' suggestions are often neglected and overlooked.
- Employees frequently request transfers to other departments.
- Manager never has time to visit the employees' work stations.
- Changes in plans and objectives are not passed on to employees.
- Communication flow is very slow, incomplete and often too late.
- The department/organization is plagued by slow decision making.
- Manager sometimes intervenes in the task without informing subordinates.
- Manager insists that all incoming/outgoing mail must first pass through him.
- Manager does not meet the deadline; often takes the office work to his home and sometimesdelays / postpones his vacation because of the work load.

If you have found one or two of the above statements in your workspace, you should look very carefully at your delegation practices and emphatically ask yourself why these conditions exist in your department / organization, and how you can utilize the above steps of applying delegation to enhance this practice.

Notes*(Place Your Notes Here)*

5- How to motivate your team

In order to have productive team, you have to keep them motivated throughout the project and above all interested in what they are doing, to achieve this follow these steps:-

1. **Explain the positive outcomes of achieving the objective if it benefits your team members:** By incorporating this team motivating step, you are putting the control of their future compensation into their own hands.
2. **Build a sense of curiosity within your team member's mindsets so that that they are interested enough to want to achieve the goals you expect:** By doing this, your team members will want to learn more. This can be achieved if you understand what excites or interests your team members.
3. **Establish a plan of action that requires cooperation between team members so that they are forced to work together to achieve that goal**: This may just mean that a project is divided into tasks that need to be accomplished by each member of the team.
4. **Challenge your team members to achieve an objective:** Make sure that they understand what you expect as a goal: Don't set them up to fail. Establish a realistic goal and provide a tool that shows their progress as they get closer to attaining that goal. For example, if you have a project that needs completing, create a chart that breaks that project into smaller goals so that, as they achieve each step, they can check it off and visualize themselves getting closer to completing the project.
5. **Create a competitive environment that will inspire your team members to achieve their goals:** For example, break your team up into smaller teams and have them each be responsible for an aspect of the complete goal. Introduce an incentive that will inspire them, but make it a friendly competition and not one that brings about hostility and back stabbing.
6. **Put your team members in control of their own destiny when instilling team motivation:** You can have an objective that needs to be met, but passing that sense of control over each of your

team members will give them the feeling that achieving the goal is something they want done.

7- **Design a tool for recognition when motivating your team:** By doing this, team members know that their individual efforts will be noticed and not lost as a team effort. This will inspire all members to do their share. If members know that they will only be rewarded and recognized as a team, they may be more inclined to hide behind the efforts of others. This in turn, may cause resentment amongst those who did all the work.

Notes*(Place Your Notes Here)*

6- How to influence your team to do what you want

What you want is coming under what you expect, coming advices are coming out from the saying "You get what you expect", here are four actions to achieve this statement.

1- **Use Parkinson's Law**: Want to know how to use expectation to persuade others to accomplish tasks 2 times, 3 times, or even many times faster? If the task requires 3 months to finish, tell them it has to be done within 3 weeks. The magic in this is that the work will be completed in a span of time based on a person's expectation of how much time is required to do it. **Parkinson's Law states "work expands so as to fill the time available for its completion."** If they cannot absolutely do it in that span of time, use another subliminal persuasion technique - the principle of comparison. Tell them that if they can produce excellent results, they will be given, let's say, a 2-week extension. They will compare the 2 time frames and may even thank you for giving them enough time! You gave them the impression that they are given a lot of time (because you've added 2 weeks to the original 3-week deadline), even when the task can take up to 3 months to finish.

2- **Be Specific**: Another great tip to maximize the power of expectation is to be as specific as possible. If you can say, "I know you're a fast writer who can turn out at least 7 quality articles within 5 hours" instead of "I know you to be a fast and efficient writer," then the results will be better and more accurate.

3- **Find Similarities and Point That Out**: To successfully influence people, find any point of similarity between you and the person you're persuading.

4- **Expect To Be Expected**: Keep in mind also that people base their expectations on various aspects such as your physical qualities, your surroundings, etc. Everyone will expect a neatly dressed and well groomed person to be wealthy and successful; that's why it pays to look good when you're persuading others. If you wear dirty clothes and have unkempt hair, you'll be treated as someone who has bad manners, and they won't expect good outcome from you. The same goes if you have an orderly and tidy home. People will expect you to be an organized person.

Notes(Place Your Notes Here)

7- How to build trust with your client

1- **Let Your Client See Your Kitchen:** When was the last time you've seen a restaurant's kitchen? We can all guess why it's not common practice to let restaurant patrons see the backend of a restaurant. What if there's food on the floor, or a cook forgot to wear a hat or hairnet?

   But imagine walking into a kitchen and seeing that it was spotless. You would most likely trust the quality of their food, right?

   Being maximally transparent also keeps you on your toes, operating at the highest-quality capacity possible at all times, knowing that your customers can walk in at any time.

   Screen-share with your clients. Show off your development tools and new hardware (if they're interested).

   Use a software or a tool that lets clients view the tasks and milestones related to their projects.

   Be as transparent as you possibly can with your operations. It builds trust with clients by showing them that you're upfront about the work you do and that you take pride in your behind-the-scenes production process.

2- **Show That You Care About Their Expenses:** Establish a relationship where your clients see that you're being a custodian of their expenses. Show them that you care about spending too much of their money.

Even if you stand to lose a bit of billable hours yourself, be vocal about something you think isn't worth the development costs. If they request a feature that you know won't move them forward with their goal, or might even be detrimental to it, tell them why and also recommend better options (even if the option is to scrap the feature).

Sacrificing billable hours for the benefit of your client's project will go a long way to building trust. This will not only lead to a better product that you can proudly display in your company's portfolio, but also says a lot about how much you care about the client's success, which is a compelling reason to continue working with you.

3- **Learn About Their Business:** You want your clients to view your work relationship like a partnership. By knowing as much as possible about their business, you stand a better chance of creating a better product for them.

The more you know about their business, the more they'll feel that you're a part of it, and the more likely they'll be encouraged to continue working with you.

You can ask them to walk you through a typical day in their office. Ask them if there are any particular pain points that they think you can solve.

If possible, try out their company's products or services to see how they work and to experience how it is being their customer.

Being knowledgeable about your client's business will give them confidence in the products you build for them.

4- **Substitute "I" for "We":** Another way to make your client feel that you're part of their business is by using "We" instead of

"I". It's a simple substitution of a pronoun that displays your vested interest in their project.

5- **Be Honest At All Times:** If you play games, you'll get caught. Don't pad hours when you feel you're working extra efficiently, and take away hours when you feel you aren't at the top of your game. Be accurate when tracking your billable hours.

Notes(Place Your Notes Here)

8- How to write effective mails to your stakeholders

1- **Write Shorter Emails:** Shorter emails increase your response rate for one reason: it is easy to write a short reply to a short email.

   While many people you email want to send a short answer, they often feel that a quick, one sentence response will come across as terse and unfriendly. The result is that they simply put the email off until they have more time to write a longer response — which is usually never.

   Short emails remove this fear because it is appropriate to reply immediately with a brief response.

2- **Reduce the Opportunity for Procrastination:** When long or unclear emails enter someone's inbox they get placed in the to-do pile because they take time to figure out and respond to. Sadly, the to-do pile usually ends up being the never-do pile.

   However, when a short, one question email comes in, it gets a response much faster.

   Make it hard for the reader to procrastinate sending you a reply.

3- **Promotion vs. Prevention:** Normally people are different in responding to promotion (touting the benefits of taking a certain action) and responding to prevention (highlighting what there is to lose from not taking a certain action).

If you aren't getting a response, then you may find success from reversing the way you phrase your request.

For example, let's say your job is to find new businesses that can partner with your company. You might not get a response if your boss is the type of person that responds to prevention statements, but you send an email saying, "This is a great opportunity. I think we should partner with company X because of A, B, and C."

However, you might find immediate success if you flip the statement towards a prevention tone such as, "This is a great opportunity. We have a lot to lose here if we don't move quickly. Company X's new product line offers a growth opportunity that we don't want to miss out on."

Determine whether the person you're emailing wants to prevent downfalls or discover new opportunities, and then adjust your message accordingly.

4- **Always Have a Purpose:** If you want a response, then your email should have a clear purpose. This applies in all situations, but it's especially helpful when reaching out to someone for the first time.
Important people are busy and they value their time, so you should always have a clear purpose for the meeting. Not only does having an event or goal help drive the conversation, also it makes the meeting feel more productive. Both parties feel a small sense of accomplishment for completing the task that was laid out at the beginning.

5- **Do the Work for Them:** When you send an unclear email, you're essentially saying to the recipient, "It's not important enough for me to figure out what the main idea of this email is, so I'm going to make you do it for me."

The main question or offer should be stated clearly and early within your email. If it's not within the first few sentences, then start over.

6- **Don't Take "No" Personally:** Everyone is busy. For most people, it's simply a matter of timing. If you catch them on a good day, then they will happily respond to you.

If they're swamped, however, then a simple "No" might be all that you get.

Don't take it to heart. In most cases, it's not a reflection of what you said.

7- **Make It a Point to Follow Up:** What if they don't respond to your email? Wait a few days and then follow up. You don't want to pester anyone, but if you give them some time and don't get a response, then there is nothing wrong with being persistent.

Recommended to wait anywhere from 3 days to a week before reaching out again. (The more busy the person is, the longer you should wait.)

8- **Send Your Message to One Person Only:** Are too many people receiving your emails? When multiple people receive the same message, the diffusion of responsibility phenomenon begins to set in. Everyone knows what needs to be done and they all assume that someone else will do it.

If you value a response to your emails, then send them to individuals instead of groups.

9- **Don't Hide Behind Email:** Pressing Send isn't the same as doing your job. The ability to collaborate and interact through the Web doesn't remove your responsibilities in the real world.

Sometimes you need to pick up the phone and get an immediate answer. Sometimes you need to meet face-to-face instead of sending an email and claiming that you "did your part."

Project Monitor and Control

The project monitor and control is the fourth phase in any project life cycle but it has different nature which is other phases starts at a point and ends at another point in the project but this phase will start once the project initiation phase starts and ends with the project closing phase ends, because the main target of it is monitoring the activities happening and controlling it to go back to the right track if any deviation.

The maximum effort of this phase is during the execution phase where most of the work is being done.

1- How to keep your eyes on your projects

No project is going as was planned because there are some unexpected events happening during the project which delay the project and take it out of the track, here are some actions you as a project manager MUST do throughout the project repetitively to keep your eyes on the project and do immediate actions if things are not going on track:-

1- **Project Meetings:** regardless this project meeting is daily like agile recommends or weekly depending on the project status but it must exist and practiced because during this project meeting you are listening to your team and their issues or complaints and it is your and only your responsibility to resolve such issues. Without having this project meeting issues will stay out there becoming bigger until become disasters which you might not be able to resolve.

2- **Individual Interview with them team:** you can't imagine how such practice will tell you about the hidden facts of the project where those facts can't be told in the project team meeting, apart from this it gives the team member more confidence and it encourages him/her to contact you anytime and just speak up.

3- **Encourage Contribution for Issues / Risks logging:** you can't see all risks / issues yourself so make sure that you encourage people to contribute with you to share risks /issues from their perspective but determine who / what / when to log an issue / risk, that is very important to keep you risk register or issue log consistent and accurate.

4- **Timely Completion on Timesheets and Tasks:** make sure that everyone in the team is updating his/her timesheet and tasks log, in this way you will have exact real status on the progress which will tell you early enough if there is any delay so you can contact that team member and try to know the reason behind the delay because he/she might need a support or training, on the other hand timesheet is very important for the payroll department.

5- **Weekly Status Report:** weekly status report is stating the progress achieved in the past week and how it is going to affect plans next week if there is any delay or priorities changes also it documents the dependencies on other parties and how this will affect the ongoing activities, in this way of reporting you are setting the expectations for the higher management and putting all stakeholders on the same page on weekly basis.

Notes(Place Your Notes Here)

2- How to manage remote teams

It is all about communications, because you do not have the team physically at your workspace it is depending on sending feedback and waiting for responses which are communications. Here are 6 tips to let the overseas communications better:-

1- **Team Building:** although the team is not exist physically in the same place but you still can be creative about having this team building over the internet by online games or by another venue which is available for both side of the teams.

2- **Build Interpersonal Relationships:** encourage the personal side between you and your team by going beyond the project scope and ask about team member's personal life or about his/her kids. Having such activities will give your credit to use later when the project goes for crisis or risky situations.

3- **Daily Standup:** it is not questionable practice, you must have daily stand up meetings for 15-30 minutes maximum to review what team has done yesterday compared to what he had to do and what he is going to do during the day.

4- **Phone Conference / Video / Web Sharing**: do not depend on mails only for communications because mail is asynchronous but Phone Conference, video or web sharing is synchronous communication which leverage effective communication between the team members to eliminate any misunderstanding might happen because of mails.

5- **Follow the Sun:** take care about your team geographical representation and try to put the tasks and activities to follow the sun so that dependencies would not be affected.

6- **Daily Summary:** get this kind of commitment from team members to summarize all activities during the day compared to what was planned stating any obstacles they faced or any dependencies affected him/her to achieve his/her tasks to be discussed again in the standup meeting.

Finally, remote team might be a blessing or a curse. If you followed above steps it will be a bless because you will have good monitoring to your remote team as if they exist beside you but if you did not follow it will be curse because the project will go away from you because the team will go around here and there doing things which are not planned.

Notes(Place Your Notes Here)

3- How to emphasize team working

Team working is one of the key success factor to any project, no one can do the whole work himself and no one can know everything. Without team working your project success is questionable big time, following ten actions to ensure team working:-

1- **The team understands the goals and is committed to attaining them**: This clear direction and agreement on mission and purpose is essential for effective team work. This team clarity is reinforced when the organization has clear expectations for the team's work, goals, accountability, and outcomes.

2- **Suitable and adoptable environment**: The team creates an environment in which people are comfortable taking reasonable risks in communicating, advocating positions, and taking action. Team members trust each other. Team members are not punished for disagreeing.

3- **Communication is open, honest, and respectful**. People feel free to express their thoughts, opinions, and potential solutions to problems. People feel as if they are heard out and listened to by team members who are attempting to understand. Team members ask questions for clarity and spend their thought time listening deeply rather than forming rebuttals while their coworker is speaking.

4- **Team members have a strong sense of belonging to the group:** They experience a deep commitment to the group's decisions and actions. This sense of belonging is enhanced and reinforced when the team spends the time to develop team norms or relationship guidelines together.

5- **Team members are viewed as unique people**: With irreplaceable experiences, points of view, knowledge, and opinions to contribute. After all, the purpose for forming a team is to take advantage of the differences. Otherwise, why would any organization approach projects, products, or goals with a team. In fact, the more that a team can bring out divergent points of view, that are thoughtfully presented and supported with facts as well as opinions, the better.

6- **Creativity, innovation, and different viewpoints are expected and encouraged**: Comments such as, "we already tried that and it didn't work" and "what a dumb idea" are not allowed or supported.

7- **The team is able to constantly examine itself and continuously improve its processes, practices, and the interaction of team members**: The team openly discusses team norms and what may be hindering its ability to move forward and progress in areas of effort, talent, and strategy.

8- **The team has agreed upon procedures for diagnosing, analyzing, and resolving team work problems and conflict:** The team does not support member personality conflicts and clashes nor do team members pick sides in a disagreement. Rather, members work towards mutual resolution.

9- **Participative leadership is practiced**: In leading meetings, assigning tasks, recording decisions and commitments, assessing progress, holding team members accountable, and providing direction for the team.

10- **Members of the team make high quality decisions together**: and they should have the support and commitment of the group to carry out the decisions made.

Notes(Place Your Notes Here)

4- How to manage lazy employee

Team members are not always stars, you will face at least once a lazy employee inside your team who is affecting the overall progress and other team members' attitude. In such situation you must take an action immediately because having this employee inside your team longer will reflect on you badly in the future throughout the project, following actions you should take to deal with such employee:-

1- **Document the situation:** Keep accurate attendance records and monitor coffee and lunch breaks. Verify if work is going undone or if a project's completion is hindered by the lazy employee's lack of performance.

2- **Confront the employee:** Once you have your evidence, talk with the employee and ask them about their absences or their poor work performance. Find out if there is a valid reason for what you perceive as laziness.

3- **Establish concrete goals and timelines for the employee's performance to improve:** Check with them often to see if things are improving. They need to understand that they risk losing their job if their performance does not start to meet your expectations.

4- **Give the employee the tools that he or she needs to get the job done**: Often, employees are not lazy, they just have inadequate supplies to do the job. Make sure computers, other equipment, documentation, needed knowledge and office supplies are adequate to do the job. Provide additional training if necessary.

5- **Encourage the employee to prioritize tasks and to maintain an organized work area**: Sometimes an employee is just overwhelmed with what needs to be done and they end up looking lazy.

6- **Meet with the employee at the end of the time period set out in your initial meeting**: Discuss any progress that has been made and any areas that still need attention. Unfortunately, this may be the time to let the person go if no improvement has been seen.

7- **Set up times for regular performance reviews with the employee:** This ensures that they will continue to excel and will not relapse into lazy habits.

Notes*(Place Your Notes Here)*

5- How to manage team conflict effectively

Team conflict one of the major reason behind project failure. That is why you have to monitor it closely and resolve it once it is clear to you in your team behaviors because for sure it will affect the outcome of your project and might cause project complete failure.

Team Conflict: defined as serious disagreements / issues over needs or goals among team members.

1- **How can you monitor conflict**? There are some triggers if happened then you can be assured that you have conflict among your team:-
   - Delay in completing the tasks and ignoring quality goals.
   - Ignoring Phone calls or e-mails.
   - Hiding information and experience which should be shared.
   - Violating meeting rules and disrespecting timings.
   - Verbal abuse or insulting others.
   - Continuous complaining about others.
   - Losing ownership and finger pointing.
   - Gossip / hostility.

   Having one or two from above triggers does not mean necessarily you have conflicts but having continuous delay in completing tasks or continuous ignoring phone and e-mail means that you might have a conflict which will affect your team and set you and you team away from "High Performance Team".

   What is the definition of "High Performance Team"?

- Works together to achieve mutual goals.
- Recognizes that each member is accountable, a team player, and committed to achieving team goals.
- Communicates effectively with each other.
- Has a balance of team members with the skills and abilities to meet mutual goals.
- Shares the joy of achievement and the pain of not meeting goals.
- Shares information, helps each other, and recognizes that the success of the group is dependent uponeach individual.
- Is able to deal with conflict.
- Understands roles and responsibilities and respects each other.
- Marches to the same tune or is aligned with goals and commitments.

By definition then, a non-productive team, or a team in conflict, does not have these traits. When conflict is not handled, it becomes poisonous. It reduces productivity, causes missed deadlines and poor quality, can impact the health of team members, and causes turnover. However, when team conflict is resolved, team members grow individually and as a team. They are better able to deal with conflict.

2- What are the reasons behind team conflict?

Conflict occurs because of an inability to address needs or goals, or because goals are unclear, unacceptable, unrealistic, or are in opposition to the parties involved.

Here are some main reasons which cause team conflict:-

- Lack of effective communication or no communication at all.
- Lack of required skills for problem solving and disability of finding the root cause.

- Lack of clarity in purpose, goals, objectives, team and individual roles.
- Poor time management.
- Lack of trust between team members.
- Lack of leadership and management.
- Lack of individual ownership of each team member.
- Team members bored, not challenged, not really interested.
- Lack of skills and abilities in team members.
- Personality conflicts.
- Personal issues.

Being able to resolve conflict effectively is a critical team skill. The manager, as leader, holds the key to helping team members resolve conflict and develop trust in each other. Without trust team members will not bond. If they do not trust each other they will not be able to deal with conflict. Conflict resolution is one of the key factors associated with committed and productive teams.

3- How can you address the team conflict?

There are 5 steps to address the conflict:-

a. **Define the problem**: You cannot solve a problem until you define it. Defining a problem is frequently the hardest part of the solution, and most of us jump into solving the problem rather than defining the problem. However, the process of defining the problem also contains the seeds of the solution.

One way to work on a problem statement is to write it down multiple times in different ways and from different perspectives. Just this exercise is beneficial for a team because it allows for different perspectives. A key to success during team interactions is first to establish how the team will operate together.

When we allow ourselves to look at the problem from different perspectives and through different statements, we can begin to agree on which statement most reflects the real problem. We might agree that the specific one of those statements is a good general description of what's going on. Each of the other statements helps us to break down the problem into more manageable chunks for work assignments. We've used a good process for problem definition, and now we have a problem statement with sub-headings. We have used a good process for problem definition and are more equipped to develop a solution.

b. **Collect Data:** The second step to addressing team conflict is to gather data on what is actually occurring. Collecting data means gathering facts that can be substantiated and proven. Opinions are just that and cannot be used. Our intent is to gather facts, which are actual observable and measurable behavior. It also means observing first-hand through meetings, teleconferencing, or video conferencing. We need to know about individual performances, who is meeting deadlines and goals, who works independently, who comes up with good ideas, who initiates, who takes on extra work or goes that extra mile, who's inside or outside of the group, who lunches together, and who are our informal leaders. We can see that this data-gathering is the manager's job and requires discretion.

Another part of data gathering is to review what you, as manager, have been doing. How do you communicate with your team? How do they communicate with each other? Are team members clear on roles and responsibilities? Have you been providing regular performance feedback to them? Have you been visible, available, and supportive? Do you "know" your employees? Do you have a good understanding of individual job roles, skills, experience, and what motivates each employee?

c. **Analyze The Data:** We have now defined the problem, and we have gathered the facts. Before we begin to analyze the data, we have to make sure of
    i. Everything we've gathered so far makes sense?
    ii. Do we have observable and verifiable facts?
    iii. Are we clear about symptoms and potential causes?
    iv. Have we separated management and employee causes and issues?

If so, we are ready to analyze.

Analyzing the data means we can diagnose what is going on with the team itself, and determine the role the manager is playing. Let's assume we've completed a self-assessment and know what you, as manager, have to do to help solve the problem. Analyze the data you have to take each expected reason from point 2 and try to ask yourself why we came to this point? What did you do to prevent this cause from occurring, let us take each reason and diagnose it:-

- **Lack of effective communication or no communication at all**
    - What kind of communications is occurring?
    - Have I established a style and/or methodology for communications to ensure that everyone on the team is updated on a regular basis? Do I have a communications plan?
    - Is it effective or non-productive?
- **Lack of required skills for problem solving and disability of finding the root cause**
    - How do we approach problems and issues?

- o Do we really address root cause or do we deal with symptoms?
- o Do we capture data as we problem-solve or is it a haphazard, uncoordinated session that does notresolve issues and does not seek input from all team members?
- **Lack of clarity in purpose, goals, objectives, team and individual roles**
  - o Do all team members understand their individual roles and the role of each team member?
  - o Do they understand how the group goals roll up to support the larger group's goals and all the way upto support Corporate group goals?

Above are some example to tell you how to think about analyzing the reasons you identified already.

As you perform your diagnosis, you develop a more precise understanding of team dynamics. Instead of just sayingI have poor communications, you can focus in on details. As you analyze each area, you can see twothings: further problem definition, and the beginnings of your plan to fix things. As manager, you have yourown skills and abilities and tools you like to use. Use whatever works for you. You might simply ask yourselfthese questions and capture your answers. A checklist may be appropriate, or a diagram, or flow chart. Yourframework or outline for your plan will depend upon you as an individual and your experience as a manager.Those factors also will determine the point when you involve your team members.

d. **Choose the best solution:** As you gather and analyze our data, you have begun to separate it into discrete areas such as communications, poor time management, etc. you are getting down to "root causes" versus symptoms. You are really defining what's wrong. With answers to questions in each area, you can focus in on distinct areas of the problem. You can work on solutions and then choose the best solution, or solutions, to implement. You will not have major issues in all areas. Plus, addressing some areas, such as leadership, role and responsibility clarification, and communications, will likely improve other areas.

How do you select the best solution? Look at each of the areas again – plus issues you've thought of. Consider what you've observed. If necessary, go out and observe some more. Write down your notes on observable behaviors. Reflect on them. Consider the impact of individual behaviors on team members, on how team members talk and work together, and how they interact with each other in meetings. Results will help you to determine which ones are the best solutions for your team's particular problems. Talk with your boss or mentor and reflect together. Let's face it. We can't always be right the first time. If we try something and it doesn't work, we can perform a "lessons-learned analysis" and try again.

e. **Implement the solution and continue to refine it:** Through the work you have already done, you have the seeds of your "get-well" plan. After you analyze the data and develop solutions, you select the best solution for your problem areas and begin to construct a plan. This plan will include actions to address each problem area, and will include a schedule for implementation with measurements. Work on one or two areas versus trying to fix everything at once.

As you develop our plan and/or begin implementation you may need help. You need to talk with your manager orto a mentor or someone trustworthy with the appropriate skills, or you could go to a class.We have to look at your management style and how it's working. You need to keep your minds open to finding the best solution and plan for your team.

The process for this is part of the solution. Thinking and considering in an ordered and systematic process is crucial to defining and solving the problem. Working together to define and correct causes of conflict is the best solution to resolve team conflict. Are there tools and aids to help teams deal with conflict quickly and effectively? Yes. In defining the problem, gathering data, analyzing that data, and selecting and implementing the best solution, you have begun to develop a list of tools and skills to use to resolve conflict. Here are other tools and skills that can help:

- Clearly articulate thoughts and ideas
- Active listening
- Give effective feedback
- Think and analyze in a methodical and systematic way
- Set clear, reasonable, achievable objectives
- Identify risks and assumptions
- Build contingencies to counter risks and assumptions
- Stick to facts and issues, not personalities or personal issues
- Take turns
- Develop the ability to work effectively as a team member
- Cross training
- Delegating and mentoring for senior employees

How do you, as a manager, help employees to develop these skills and tools? One way is through modeling the behavior desired. Another is through coaching. Another is to directly state what is required. Still another is through training. As a manager, we can work with our team to develop a process that is acceptable for conflictresolution. Belowis an example of a simple conflict resolution process.

Conflict Resolution Steps

Step 1: The first step is for individuals to try to resolve the conflict with each other. You might need to perform somecoaching first. Or, you may need to listen to each side independently. This will help each individual to sort outtheir thoughts and feelings before the one-on-one. Being able to resolve conflict with each other helps individualsto learn how to confront each other, clearly state the issue, listen to each other, and work together to finda mutually acceptable solution. The benefit is that individuals learn a highly critical skill for now and thefuture, and become more valuable team members.

Step 2: If the two individuals are not successful with a one-on-one meeting, you may need to intercede. If you have notalready met with each person, you would do that first. Then you would bring the two people together with cleargoals and an expected outcome. There should be rules or guidelines as to how the meeting will be conductedand how they are expected to behave. This latter step about behavior may not berequired in all instances, but you all know that sometimes you have to be very explicit about what will and will not be tolerated.

Step 3: If Step 2 doesn't work, or if the conflict involves us as manager, the next step is to involve Human Resources.Human Resource people generally have excellent skills and/or have contacts with people who specialize inmediation and conflict resolution for conflict situations requiring this level of expertise.

4- **Excellent Tips for maturing dealing with conflict resolution**

Successful Project Managers Roadmap

- Attack the problem, not the person
- Focus on what can be done, not on what can't be done
- Encourage different points of view and honest dialogue
- Express feelings in a way that does not blame
- Accept ownership appropriately for all or part of the problem
- Listen to understand the other person's point of view before giving your own
- Show respect for the other person's point of view
- Solve the problem while building the relationship

Notes *(Place Your Notes Here)*

6- How to manage project changes

There are 4 actions you have to do to manage / control / minimize project changes:-

1. **Get the whole team involved:** let everybody in the team know what you are going to deliver exactly by sharing SOW (Statement of work), schedule, Requirements Specifications even the acceptance criteria. Having this knowledge sharing will help them to identify changes or find brilliant solution for requested changes by spending less effort.

2. **Defend Scope:** train you people to defend the scope and never give the client any promises until they come back to you to discuss it in details and find other solutions without changing the scope and if no other solution then go for the change.

3. **Enforce CR (Change Request) Process:** make sure that every change will go through CR process to evaluate the impact (use relevant team member for that) and approve it then go for implementation.

4. **Don't do the work until getting the permission:** do not ever give informal approvals or take handshaking permission and do the work based on it, because if things went wrong and who approved it informally took his word back they will never get you paid for the work you have done.

Notes(Place Your Notes Here)

7- How to prevent your project from scope creep

Scope creep: - Is increasing the scope without rebasing the cost or/and schedule.

Any project is exposed to an extent to scope creep if we did not give high attention to control it, and here are 7 tips you have to apply from day one in your project to prevent / control scope creep:-

1. **Define Scope**: - make sure that you have defined scope before project starts and not after because based on that scope definition you will baseline you cost and schedule and apply your required skills analysis then request for team members.

2. **Log Change**: - you can't say no to changes on projects but it must go through defined process which will ensure <u>documenting</u>, <u>evaluating</u> the impact (Cost / Schedule) and <u>approving</u> it through your Change Control Board (CCB).

3. **Rebaseline**: - after approving to include the change you have to rebaseline because most of the time this change will increase cost or schedule and make sure that you will communicate the new baseline to all stakeholders to get the buy-in from all of them and set the expectations as well.

4. **Adjust**: - after setting new baseline you will have to adjust the plan either by crashing resources or Fast Tracking, keeping in mind the risk increased by the last method.

5- **Monitor:** you have to monitorthe change effect,"Everything is going ok?" You have to get that answer from getting more in touch with you team members and try to get the truth and do not get satisfied by one or two answers from one or two team members "Everything is ok boss", the fact may be not, so try to get the truth without falling also in the micro management trap and try to balance.

6- **CCB:** if it came to the point of having many approved changes so ask CCB to set the priorities so you can plan according to the customer satisfaction and priorities.

7- **Avoid:** strictly avoid acceptance of corridor talking or discussion results in a new change, every single change must go through the process and can't be approved by handshaking.

Notes(Place Your Notes Here)

8- How to use Pareto Chart to improve quality

Pareto Chart Definition: it is statistical representation for the frequency of occurrence for specific set of categories or classes, represented by bars where X-Axis is representing the frequency and Y-Axis is representing the categories / classes (*Pareto Chart is special version of Histogram Graph*)

How to use it?

As described in the definition it is representing the frequency of categories, these categories can be your project issues' categories like Page Slowness, Exceptions, UI Complaints, Data manipulation and Database locking.

There are eight steps to create "Pareto Chart":-

1- **Develop a list of problems, items or causes to be compared:** which we mentioned above, but it can be anything you see your project is suffering from.

2- **Develop a standard measure for comparing the items:** it can be
   a. How often it occurs: frequency (our example will use frequency)
   b. How long it takes: time
   c. How many resources it uses: cost

3- **Choose a timeframe for collecting the data:** start observing the system in defined timeframe, all collected data must be in this timeframe.

4- **Grouping and calculating the weight:** Tally, for each item, how often it occurred (or cost or total time it took). Then, add these amounts to determine the grand total for all items. Find the percent of each item in the grand total by taking the sum of the item, dividing it by the grand total and multiplying by 100.

Category	Frequency	Percentage (%)
Page Slowness Complaints	10	15
Unhandled Exceptions	20	30
Bad UI Experience	5	7
Data Issues	30	45
Database locking	2	3
Totals	67	100 %

5- **Calculate the accumulative Percentages:** List the items being compared in decreasing order of the measure of comparison: e.g., the most frequent to the least frequent. The cumulative percent for an item is the sum of that item's percent of the total and that of all the other items that come before it in the ordering by rank.

Category	Frequency	Percentage (%)	Accumulative Percentage (%)
Data Issues	30	45	45
Unhandled Exceptions	20	30	75
Page Slowness Complaints	10	15	90
Bad UI Experience	5	7	97
Database locking	2	3	100

6- **Draw the chart:** List the items on the horizontal axis of a graph from highest to lowest. Label the left vertical axis with the numbers (frequency, time or cost), then label the right vertical axis with the cumulative percentages (the cumulative total should equal 100 percent). Draw in the bars for each item.

7- **Draw the line:** Draw a line graph of the cumulative percentages. The first point on the line graph should line up with the top of the first bar. Excel offers simple charting tools you can use to make your graphs, or you can do them with paper and pencil.

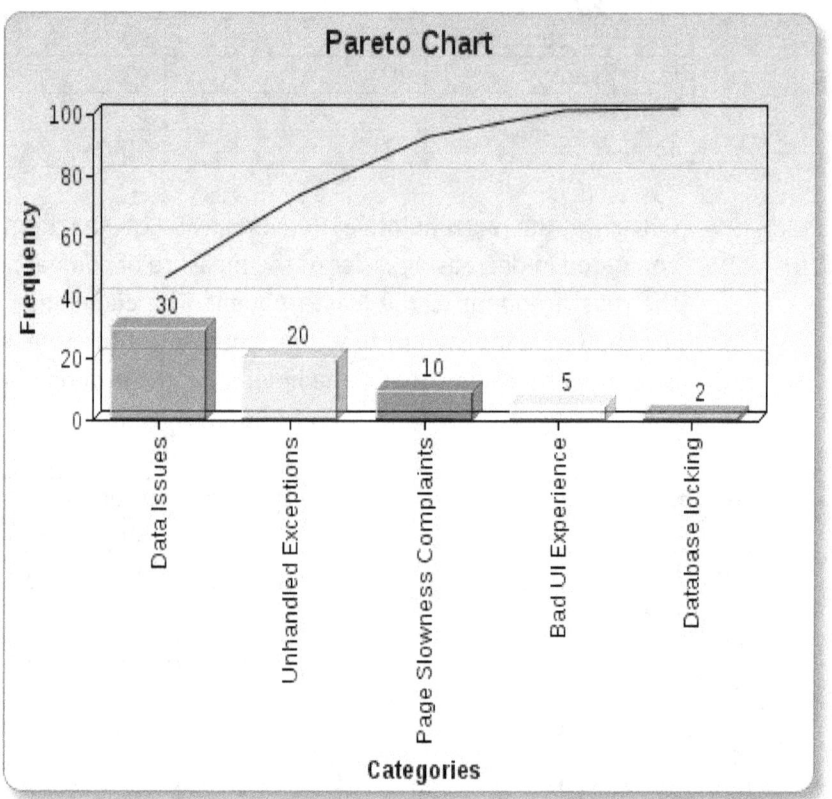

8- **Decide the highest frequency categories:** Analyze the diagram by identifying those items that appear to account for most of the difficulty. Do this by looking for a clear breakpoint in the line graph, where it starts to level off quickly. If there is not a breakpoint, identify those items that account for 50 percent or more of the effect.

After tackling highest frequency categories you have to repeat above steps from No. 3 to see who much the resolution was effective to reduce the frequency of the issues.

There is one important fact saying resolving 20 % of the causes will resolve 80% of the issues (80/20 rule), Pareto chart is helping you to apply this fact because "Pareto Chart" is focusing on the frequency of issues not in severity.

Notes(Place Your Notes Here)

9- How to manage project issues effectively

You will be receiving issues continuously as long as the project is progressing on, you can't get rid of the issues, so you will need to manage it effectively."Effectively" here means resolving the issue before it comes bigger and without wasting your and your team efforts. To do to here are 8 actions:-

1- **Create Log:** a log must be created to register all issues and this log must be easily accessible and easily to manager.

2- **Log Issues:** make sure that issues are logged once it appear but put rules there for <u>who will log</u>? <u>What to log</u>? <u>When to log</u>? These questions' answers will define the rules for anyone when issues come, in this way you will ensure the consistency, accuracy and accountability in issues logging.

3- **Assess & Set Priority:** once the issue is logged someone responsible and experienced must assess the impact and evaluate it then report it to you then you will have to set the priority of that issue because your team might be working already on other issues which less in priority.

4- **Assign:** after assessing and setting the priority it will be easy to you to assign the issue to someone who is experienced in resolving such issues. Assigning must specify person and time to close the issue.

5- **Monitor**: after assigning you must monitor the progress to see if we are going to close the issue on time, and if not you will have to escalate promptly and properly. **Promptly** means with no delay or any traits off. **Properly** means select the proper time to escalate and focus on the issue not on persons.

6- **Reassess**: after first assessment and setting the priority you might decide to delay this issue and not to assign it now, if this is the case then you must keep your reassessment practice because the impact might change due to project or environmental changes.

7- **Approve**: after marking the issue to "Resolved" you must verify it either by experience people or by customer himself.

8- **Close out:** after approval of resolving the issue get it out from the log and keep it in a history along with the resolution to help you in next project / phases or other people in your organization.

Notes *(Place Your Notes Here)*

10- How to use and apply Earned Value Management

Earned Value Management (EVM) Definition

Earned Value Management (EVM) helps project managers to measure project performance. It is a systematic project management process used to find variances in projects based on the comparison of worked performed and work planned. EVM is used on the cost and schedule control and can be very useful in project forecasting. The project baseline is an essential component of EVM and serves as a reference point for all EVM related activities. EVM provides quantitative data for project decision making.

To use EVM you need to calculate three types of data:-

1. **Planned Value (PV):** the authorized budget for a planned piece of work. Sometimes called Budgeted Cost of Work Scheduled (BCWS).
2. **Earned Value (EV):** the authorized budget for work actually completed. Sometimes called Budgeted Cost of Work Performance (BCWP).
3. **Actual Cost (AC):** the costs actually incurred in completing the work actually achieved (the work as measured by the EV above) Sometimes called Actual Cost of Work Performed (ACWP).

To illustrate how to calculate above data on real example, consider below tasks:-

Task Name	Start Date	End Date	Planned Cost to complete the task	Current(Actual) Completed Percentage	Actual Cost spent to achieve the completed percentage

Task 1	1/1/2013	1/1/2013	100$	100 %	110$
Task 2	2/1/2013	5/1/2013	500$	50 %	300$
Task 3	3/1/2013	5/1/2013	200$	66 %	100$

Consider that today is End of 4/1/2013, so we are expecting the 100% of Task1, 75% of task 2 and 66% of task 3.

Now let us calculate each type of data

Planned Value (PV): 100 % of Task1 + 75 % of Task 2 + 66 % of task 3 = (1.0 * 100$) + (0.75 * 500$) + (0.66 * 200$) = 607$

Earned Value (EV): 100 % of Task 1+ 50 % of Task 2 + 66 % of task 3 = (1.0 * 100$) + (0.5 * 500$) + (0.66 * 200$) = 482$

Actual Cost (AC): Cost spent to achieve the completed percentage for each task = 110$ + 300$ + 100$ = 510$

Having above data only is not beneficial at all until it is used to represent the variances in the project which will tell you how much you are ahead or behind schedule and over or under budget.

To calculate how much your project has variance in schedule you need to calculate:-

Schedule Variance (SV): it is telling you how much in value your schedule is varied from planned value

SV = EV – PV = 482$ - 607$ = - 125$

If SV is positive value then it means you are ahead the schedule by this value, and vice versa if it negative value then it means you are behind schedule by this value in other words you need to compensate this value in your schedule to make SV = 1 which means your schedule is on track.

Schedule Performance Index (SPI): it acts like percentage or rate to describe how your schedule is behaving in terms of ahead or behind schedule.

SPI = EV / PV = 482 / 607 = 0.79

If SPI is greater than one then you are ahead the schedule and it is less than 1 then you are behind schedule.

A great use for SPI is the "Trend Analysis" which depends on the calculated values of SPI at different points of time during the project like each month, so after 3- 4 months you can draw a graph which will tell you the trend in your project is either you are covering up and your SPI is going high to one or you are going more late and you SPI is going more below 1.0 for each month.

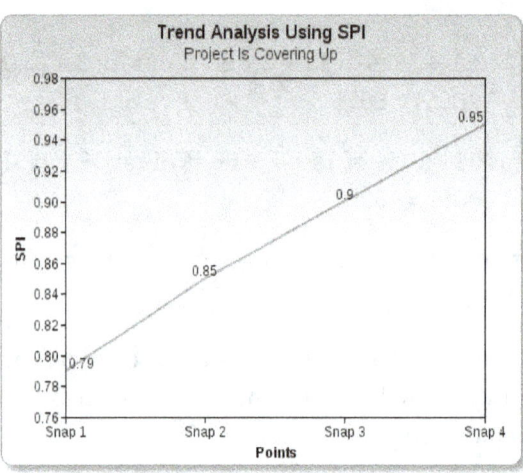

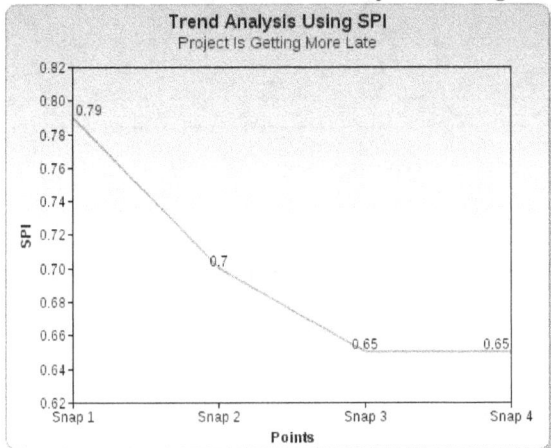

Using above calculation and figures you can know how your project is behaving and how it will continue, but schedule is not necessary reflecting cost meaning being behind schedule does not mean necessarily being over budget, so let us talk about cost analysis:-

Cost Variance (CV): it is telling how much more / less you spent on the achieved work.

CV = EV – AC = 482$ - 510$ = - 28$

If CV is positive then it means you save this amount of money and if it is negative so it means you spent this amount of money as extra to achieve this work in other words you are over budget by this amount of money.

Cost Performance Index (CPI): it acts like percentage or rate to describe how your cost/budget is behaving in terms of over or off budget.

CPI = EV / AC = 482/510 = 0.94

If CPI is greater than one then you are off budget and it is less than 1 then you are over Budget and you need to find a solution to compensate this unplanned extra money spent.

You can use the same idea of "Trend Analysis" to judge on your project trend in terms of cost control.

Notes*(Place Your Notes Here)*

11- How to forecast your project using Earned Value Management

Using EVM you can forecast your project in terms of variance in schedule and cost and needed speed or cost reduction to finish on time and on budget.

Let us define new terms which will be used to calculate forecasting which is

Budget at Completion (BAC): is the total budget allocated to the project.

Now let us start forecasting your project:-

Estimate at Completion (EAC): is the estimated cost of the project at the end of the project.

It has two formulas:-

EAC = BAC / CPI (you should use this formula if you are expecting that your CPI is going to continue fixed from now until end of the project)

EAC = AC + BAC – EV (you should use this formula if your previous variances showed as anomaly, but now it is settled down)

Considering below example:-

Task Name	Start Date	End Date	Planned Cost to complete the task	Current(Actual) Completed Percentage	Actual Cost spent to achieve the completed percentage
Task 1	1/1/2013	1/1/2013	100$	100 %	110$
Task 2	2/1/2013	5/1/2013	500$	50 %	300$
Task	3/1/2013	5/1/2013	200$	66 %	100$

3					

Calculating EAC for our example

Formula 1: EAC = 800 / 0.94 = 851$

Formula 2: EAC = 510 + 800 – 482 = 828$ (you can notice that you need less money extra because previous variances were anomaly but now it is settled down, but in formula one it continuing in delaying by the same rate from the point we started calculation).

Variance at Completion (VAC): is the variance on the total budget at the end of the project.

VAC = BAC – EAC.

Using formula 1 for EAC -> VAC = 800 - 851 = -51$ (Over Budget).

Using formula 2 for EAC-> VAC = 800 - 828 = -28$ (Over Budget).

To Complete Performance Index (TCPI): To complete Cost Performance Indicator is an index showing the efficiency at which the resources on the project should be utilized for the remainder of the project.

TCPI = (BAC – EV) *(work left to do)* / (BAC – AC) *(money left)* = (800 – 482) / (800 – 510) = 1.09.

From above result you can understand that your team should be at SPI = 1.09 in achieving their task to finish on time.

Notes*(Place Your Notes Here)*

12- How to assess / measure your project status and creation action plan

One of the key reasons that projects can fail is due to the decline of communication, which also leads to the team members not being heard. Therefore, the best way to assess the current situation is to establish and meet the team's needs.

Assuming that you have been given a project which is already late or you started the project but due to lake of knowledge and experience of the team members the project is behind schedule big time now, not only this but you have a team with low morale because they spent a lot of overtime but still the project is behind schedule.

Now, having above situation will require you to stop a bit to assess the status, if it continued like this you would not be able to finish the project on time and even not finish at all especially with current team morale. There is a standard process to turn the project around:-

1- Stop the current progress and begin a re-planning effort.
2- Determine the progress made to date and estimate the workand durations remaining.
3- Determine impact to the other project management plans(cost, schedule, risk, communications, etc.)
4- Get approval from Sponsor, stakeholders and ICC.
5- Re-publish the plan and reset expectations.

There are many variations to those steps, but in essence, that is what isrequired to begin to turn around a project. If step three is surprising,understand from a project management standpoint, a plan consists ofmuch more than just a schedule.

Now, you put the project in the right track and prepared the suitable environment for the project success by resetting the constraint and re-planning efforts but you did not resolve the morale issue, still your team is pissed off and not motivated at all to offer you more work. For that you have to spend more effort to identify the remaining tasks which are on the critical path and do some reassigning actions so all tasks on the critical path are assigned to people who can be negotiated and motivated back by paying more through overtime hours.

Such project will need extra effort of monitor and control activities from you because the chance of re-planning and setting another expectations will not be given to you again.

Notes*(Place Your Notes Here)*

13- How to select appropriate management style throughout the project

There are several different types of management styles when it comes to managing in the workplace and choosing the right type of style to lead with could have a big impact in terms of how your staff produces for you. But knowing the four different leadership styles in management does not mean that you can simply pick one and then that is going to work because you are then in essence trying to fit a square peg into a round hole. In most cases, the traits of the staff that you are managing will help to define the management styles you will use, something blending a combination of the different categories.

1. **Autocratic Management Style:** An autocratic manager makes decisions without the consultation of others, instead serving as a dictator type in communicating orders because they like to be in control of situations.
   - **Advantages**: This style of management leads to :-
     A. Work getting done on time because there are less people involved in the decision making process.
     B. Work getting done as you expect because there is one decision maker, you.
   - **Disadvantages:** The problem with this type of management style is that :-
     A. The staff are going to eventually lost motivation working in an environment where they have no say.
     B. Employee turnover is likely to run high as they move on to other opportunities where they can have an impact.
   - **When to apply:** For situations or events where an on the spot decision needs to be made or you believe that team is not mature yet to take decision where the case of beginning of the project, this type of leadership can serve a purpose, but trying to have an autocratic style of management in place for

long periods of time is just going to lead to headaches for all involved.

2- **Democratic Management Style:** A democratic manager is willing to share work with his staff by delegating it to get the job done. You are banking on the competency of your team to get the job done on time and to have it done correctly.
   - **Advantages**: This style of management leads to :-
     A. Employees love this type of management style in business because they feel involved and part of the process.
     B. Their job performance is likely to be better than in an autocratic setting, though giving them the authority to do the work may lead some to rely on other to bear the brunt of the work on the project. Also, depending on what type of work it is.
     C. Employees may feel like the work is being pushed off on them because you as a manager don't feel like doing it.
   - **Disadvantages:** The problem with this type of management style is that :-
     A. Getting too many people involved in the project or process could slow the work down.
     B. It could also mean less time for you to concentrate on your work as your team asks questions and waits on your answers before proceeding to the next steps.
   - **When to use:** The democratic style is most effective when the leader needs the team to buy into or have ownership of a decision, plan, or goal, or if he or she is uncertain and needs fresh ideas from qualified teammates. It is not the best choice in an emergency situation, when time is of the essence for another reason or when teammates are not informed enough to offer sufficient guidance to the leader.

3- **Participative Management Style:** Also sometime known as consultative management style, this decision making style in management revolves around getting lots of feedback from your staff before coming to a conclusion and making a decision.

- **Advantages:** This style of management leads to :-
  A. This means that the process can take a bit longer as there are more voices to be heard, but getting a consensus on major decisions can lead to buy in from those who might otherwise have been opposed to the implementation of such changes.
- **Disadvantages:** The problem with this type of management style is that :-
  A. The downside to this style of management and leadership is that employees may feel that you don't value their opinion or are too stubborn if after all of the feedback is received you go off and make the decision in your own without incorporating any of their feedback.
- **When to use:** If you are going to make company or departmental policy changes, this type of style can make the team feel involved and more apt to go with the flow of whatever changes are coming down. This style also works well for brainstorming sessions as you work on new product ideas or marketing promotions.

4- **Laissez Faire Management Style:** In this leadership management style, the team is given the freedom to complete the job or tasks in any way they deem it should be done. It is a hands off approach at the management level in terms of direction, but the manager is there to answer questions and provide guidance as needed.
- **Advantages:** This style of management leads to :-
  A. This is a good way to help develop individual contributors into leaders which is only going to serve to make your team stronger ion the long run.
- **Disadvantages:** The problem with this type of management style is that :-
  A. It can lead to conflict on the team is some employees try to assume the role as a leader in the interim or to dictate to others how their work should be done.

- **When to use:** you can use this management styles when you feel comfortable about the maturity of the team members and the harmony between them and their ideas, because they will interact between each other too much.

Finally, you can see there are many different management styles and each of them can serve a purpose depending on the type of business and environment you are in as well as the situation. The most effective management styles are those which you can take bits and pieces from to then combine with your own management style to create a good working environment for all involved.

Notes*(Place Your Notes Here)*

14- How to manage difficult situations by persuasion techniques

Persuasion techniques are essential to apply in any field / position where you face clients, as dealing with an irrational customer is one of the toughest situations you can tackle. How do you exactly alleviate the fury of a client who is livid because of something you, the service or product, or your company failed to perform? This is where influence and persuasion techniques may come in handy.

Because facing the clients is not a walk in the park, there will be times when you will be shouted at, and even hurled harsh words by clients who are not satisfied. Don't be alarmed. This is a normal situation. And being so, there are ways to rise above them so that you don't break down, too.

1- **Find out the main source**: First, find out what the client is angry about. Is he complaining about your service? Is he unclear about certain points in the agreement or the product? Did the problem come from you or did it spring out of his frustration over something he misunderstood? What are his sentiments exactly?

    You can find this out by being calm with the client, no matter how irritable he is. Ask politely what the problem is and request that he explain it to you. Don't interrupt and try to defend yourself or correct him while he explains. Wait for him to finish and then enumerate all your responses to his problems.

2- **Warp up the problem and commit to resolve it in one word** : Often, the customer does not really want to know exactly what you are doing to rectify the situation, only that you tell him that steps are being undertaken to correct it, and when precisely this is expected to be solved. One thing clients hate most is continuously waiting for solutions that are not certain to happen.

3- **Join his mood**: When you have figured out what he needs, level with him. Building rapport with your client is one of the best ways to get into a straight conversation with him without the flare-ups. This means adopting his current mood. If he is angry, let him know that you understand hisfeelings. If he is frustrated, empathize. Clients appreciate people who they know feel theirpain. When you have succeeded in this, you can expect to have a much calmer discussionright after.

4- **Put yourself in client's shoes**:Don't say something like "I'm sorry for that. I'm already on it." Instead, say something like "Iunderstand that you are angry now. I will feel the same if I were you. Rest assured that Iwill do everything in my power to correct this matter as soon as possible. I will constantlyupdate you of the developments as I progress."

Handling alivid customer is not so difficult if you know how to level with people. Think ofit this way. If you were in his shoes, you would be feeling the same way, right? How wouldyou want the other person to face you then? That should always be your guiding strategy.

Build rapport with the use of proper persuasion techniques and, together, seek solutions.**No issue has ever been solved by an argument**.

Notes(Place Your Notes Here)

15- How to manage your project when it is late

Any project has probability to get late due to different reasons like lack of resource in the middle of the project, bad estimations, used technology was not selected properly or team is not performing well as expected.

Regardless why your is late, you have to take immediate actions to return back your project on track and on budget as much as you can, and here are 5 actions you can perform to do so:-

1- **Bring the team together:** you and your team have to face the fact, prepare a list of all outstanding activities and risks which converted to issue because they were not resolved on time and due that we are getting late because we spent extra time to resolved those issues. Talk it out, describe the status very clearly so all the team will sense the problem and consequently they will be in your side.

2- **Ask why we get here:** try to know why we got late, why we have outstanding activities try to know the main cause, this will help you identifying the right actions to resolve the problems.

3- **Listen to solutions:** let you team to tell you solutions or workarounds which will compensate the wasted time in past activities, you might hear from them new technology which will save time in coming activities, merging some activities together to be done in one shot or swapping some activities between the team members due to past experience so they can finish it earlier. Finally you will find solutions through your team. In some cases the only solution available is crashing resources which will affect the cost on the other hand.

4- **Communicate Formally:** Do not ever hide that you are late, let stakeholders, senior management and business users know your status but not only a status it must be along with solutions. In this way they will be in your side supporting you to get back on track.

5- **Rebaeline:** if solutions were not very helpful to contain the delay and deliver in the same previously determined deadline, so you have to rebaseline either the schedule to be extended or the scope to be reduced to the most priority if the deadline is very critical.

Notes(Place Your Notes Here)

16- How to sort it out if you lied

There are difficult situations throughout the project where you can't remain honest with a client. Whatever the circumstances, the project manager may feel it would be better to not reveal all of the information or not tell the complete truth. Inevitably, however, the client will know sooner or later. Oftentimes, project managers will think that it is their burden to bear when a project is off track. They may withhold information and try to fix it themselves. What they forget is that it is not always their job to fix it! Even if he or his team are the main reason behind the delay but the client must be involved in the tradeoff decisions that come with bringing a project back into compliance. Sharing the whole story and the current status with the client ensures client's support to you and your team. There are some simple steps to follow when a client finds out that the truth has not been told.

- Formal apologize must be sent.
- Tell the client or the sponsor the whole story and whatever you hide before, including why you chose to withhold the information. Emphasize on that it is not an excuse, but an explanation.
- Acknowledge that you may have lost the client's trust and you will do whatever it takes to regain the trust through action, not empty promises.
- After the acknowledgment, be quiet and listen. Give the client or sponsor time to process the information and look to them for the instructions on how to proceed.

There may have been a perfectly valid reason to withhold information or to not to tell the truth—or at least at the time you thought there was a good reason. In the unfortunate circumstance when you have not completely told the truth, be prepared for the fallout. Any time integrity, honor, or morals are called into question, it can be difficult to deal with. Keep in mind that you created the situation, however, and you must resolve it.

Successful Project Managers Roadmap

A project manager's role is to bring chaos to order, blurred vision to clear reality, and disorganization to harmony. It is a project manager's role to plan, execute, validate, and complete projects. This responsibility includes reporting progress. Many project managers will be tempted to not tell the truth if the project is slightly behind schedule or slightly over budget. They begin to hope that it will turn around. Instead, slightly behind becomes greatly behind, and a small issue grows into a large issue. To avoid this, a good project m reports the exact progress. The moment a project goes off track, the project manager should ensure that everyone is aware that it is off track and understands what needs to be accomplished to get back on track. This has to be carried out with action and communications, not hope and prayer.

Notes*(Place Your Notes Here)*

17- How to prevent your project from failing

Any project has a probability to fail, here are some actions to prevent your project from failure:-

1- **Use the right approach:** the right approach is according to the project's circumstances and customer nature for example if your customer is not very clear about the final product specifications and business requirements then make sure that you divided you project into small iterations and get approval from the customer for each iteration, in this approach you will ensure that you are building the right product and getting feedback sooner as much as you can, finally you must study your customer, environment and stakeholders very preciously and select the appropriate approach.

2- **Get the best team you can afford:** make sure that you spent enough time in "Required Skills Analysis" activity, try to get the best team matching the results from the analysis because having such team will ensure high quality results in less time. If you can't get the best team to be allocated all the time try to have experienced people part time to check and make sure that you and your team are going on the right track.

3- **Plan to fail:** as mentioned above, there is no project with no probability to fail so you with your team must identity all risks might affect the project and build your contingency plan to mitigate those risks, go and ask for 25% from you baseline budget extra for contingency which will keep you in the safe side.

4- **Keep everybody on the same page:** from day one, from kickoff meeting keep this practice alive "Keep everybody on the same page" everybody must know if he should know this piece of information, having this knowledge sharing and transparency between all stakeholders and team members ensures full co-operative attitude for project ownership and success.

Notes *(Place Your Notes Here)*

Project Closing

The Project Closure Phase is the fifth and last phase in the project life cycle. In this phase, you will formally close your project and then report its overall level of success to your sponsor.

Project Closure involves handing over the deliverables to your customer, passing the documentation to the business, cancelling supplier contracts, releasing staff and equipment, and informing stakeholders of the closure of the project.

After the project has been closed, a Post Implementation Review is completed to determine the project's success and identify the lessons learned.

The first step taken when closing a project is to create a Project Closure Report. It is extremely important that you list every activity required to close the project within this Project Closure report, to ensure that project closure is completed smoothly and efficiently. Once the report has been approved by your sponsor, the closure activities stated in the report are actioned.

Between one and three months after the project has been closed and the business has begun to experience the benefits provided by the project, you need to complete a Post Implementation Review. This review allows the business to identify the level of success of the project and list any lessons learned for future projects.

1- How to avoid project closing pitfalls

Sometime we as project manager do not prepare ourselves for closing the project, we focus much on delivering the project to the client and meet the deadline and while doing so we are dropping a lot of things which will be impossible to get it done at this stage for example status report. So here are some actions to protect you and avoid being there alone closing the project with no support:-

1- **Make sure of existence of input of this stage:** you can refer to PMBok Guide to know what are the needed inputs for this stage for example (Performance Results, Project Progress, Project Logs, Deliverables), having all of those documents ready will make it easy to enter this stage with need to external support or internal support from your team which might be released already to another project.

2- **Get use acceptance:** you can't say we can closed the project out by just delivering the project and having client using it, you must get the client acceptance of the project, in this way you protect yourself and your company from any complaints on features which were already approved but client wants to change it, if client signed on the acceptance he can't cheat on it.

3- **Get final status report:** final status report is depending on the regularly status report delivered during the project, so make sure that everyone sent his status report because you will need them to prepare the final one.

4- **Get your final documentations:** combine all signed off documents together because you might need it at later stage for next phase or some projects are put on hold for some reasons.

5- **Celebrate:** do not miss this action, it is very important to gather with your team and celebrate the success of delivering the project. In this way team members feel that company treats them as human beings not just resources on a project. It motivates people and increase the loyalty to the company.

6- **Connect with your team:** keep in touch with your team from time to time, they might be your team again in coming projects, having this relationships make it easy managing next project so get the benefit from current project to next ones.
7- **WIFM:** to let people listen to you more and be keen to continue in the project if we are just closing phase one is WIFM (What is in it for me?), tell each team member how this project is all about for him, how it will improve his career path in the company and how it will enrich his CV.

Notes(Place Your Notes Here)

2- How to close your project effectively

A project has a beginning (Project Start-up) a middle (the iterative loop of Planning, Managing, Controlling, Reporting and Re-planning) and an end (Project Closure). This may be stating the obvious but we can probably all think of projects that have either gone on since time immemorial or simply faded away. Without senior management involvement there is no one to pull the plug on resources. Such projects enter a downward spiral in that they are seen to be a farce and soon everyone apart from the Project Manager (who feels they must carry on because they haven't been told to bring the project to a close) stops engaging with it or taking an active part. Turning up to a meeting that no one else attends is not the way to find out a project has finished. The project should be formally closed to ensure that:

- The users/customers have formally accepted all outcomes
- Operational procedures are in place
- The handover to operational staff has been completed
- Documentation and reference material is in place
- Any further actions and recommendations are documented and disseminated
- The results are disseminated to relevant people
- There are no loose ends

Project closure can be a very hectic time when reporting is on a daily (or even more frequent) basis and the manager is working at a much lower level of detail than previously (probably with itemized check-lists) to ensure that all loose ends are tied up but planning for this phase must commence much earlier on.

Actions you must take while closing your project:

1- **Handing Over The Project:** The end of the project is also the start of routine use of the outcomes. The handover to staff who will carry out normal operations must also be planned so that those staff feel ownership of the project outcomes and are ready to champion them.
2- **Lessons Learned:** All projects should document their lessons learned. In considering what types of lessons may be learned projects tend to fall into two types:
    - the project that is expected to achieve an outcome – the achievement being the reason the project is started
    - the project that is started to enable the organization, or the external funder, or similar organizations to learn – a feasibility project, proof of concept, or a project where a methodology is being tested

The success of the first type of project is dependent upon the outcome being achieved. If it is forecast that the outcome cannot be achieved to an acceptable quality there is little point in continuing to expend resource on it.

The success of the second type of project is the learning that comes out of it. If the end outcome cannot be achieved the project can still be a success if it shows why the outcome cannot be achieved or, that the outcome cannot be achieved in the way that the project was attempting to achieve it. It is also a success if the lessons learned along the way enable others to avoid similar pitfalls or mistakes. The success of such a project is more dependent on the quality of knowledge management and dissemination than on final outcome or product. If such a project achieves the desired outcome that it was testing then that is a bonus.

Such projects require particular attention and focus on the learning aspect. When things go wrong there is a natural tendency to focus on why. When things go well, there is less of an imperative to identify and record why it is going well.

A 'Lessons Learned' report gathers all information that may be useful to other projects. It documents what went well and what went badly and why. It describes methods used to estimate, to plan, to manage and control the project and how effective/efficient they were. It contains any recommendations for future projects to either take up, or avoid, ways of working and should contain some measurement of how much effort was required to produce the various products or process changes.

The Issues and Risk logs will be of immense value in producing this report. A further technique is to interview various stakeholders and members of the Project Team, Project Board and User Group to ask for their opinions.

Notes(Place Your Notes Here)

www.ingramcontent.com/pod-product-compliance
Lightning Source LLC
LaVergne TN
LVHW060155080526
838202LV00052B/4156